Gurdji

A Beginner's Guide

How Changing the Way We React To Misplacing Our Keys Can Transform Our Lives

Gil Friedman

Yara Press
Arcata, California

Are you ready for self-transformation?

Many spiritual teachers promise transformation, but Georges Ivanovitch Gurdjieff delivers. Gurdjieff (1872-1949) was born in Alexandropol on the border of Russia and Turkey. A spiritual seeker in his youth, he spent twenty years traveling in Asia and the Middle East while developing his revolutionary system of personal transformation.

Gurdjieff then settled in Moscow and started forming groups in both Moscow and St. Petersburg. Gurdjieff's teachings contain many concepts and, taken together, are referred to as the Work. The idea behind the Work is that our first birth is our physical body, which is all we need to get through life. But we are capable of developing into something higher, just as an acorn can stay an acorn and die or develop into an Oak Tree, we can develop into something higher. And whereas other methods often require the student to go to a monastery, sanctuary, or to retreats to separate from ordinary life, the Work uses our ordinary experiences in life as the material we work on for our development.

These ordinary experiences are not some interruption to our lives, but exactly the material we need to work with. This work can only be done by intentional efforts. All mechanical efforts are useless. The Work emphasizes that many of us are in negative states without realizing it. And if there is any mantra in the Work it might be that we have the right not to be negative. The end result of our development is that we develop ourselves to a higher level, so we react differently to the events that transpire in our lives, more consciously and less mechanically.

Often challenging and even esoteric, Gurdjieff offers a radically original version of man and his potential for self-development. *Gurdjieff, A Beginner's Guide: How Changing the Way We React To Misplacing Our Keys Can Transform Our Lives* is a beginning guide to the teachings of Gurdjieff. Practical and eminently readable, it leads the reader through some of the main concepts necessary for self-transformation.

ISBN 0-913038-27-X

Readers interested in obtaining copies of this book or any other book by Gil Friedman can contact him at:

Yara Press
1735 J Street
Arcata, CA 95521
Tel. (707) 822-5001

gilfriedman1@gmail.com
www.GilFriedman.com

Other books by Gil Friedman

The Goldwater Calendar: Time for a Change???

How to Buy and Sell a Used Car in Europe

How to Conduct Your Own Divorce in England and Wales and a Guide to the Divorce Laws

A Dictionary of Love

Love Notes: Quotations from the Heart
An expanded version of A Dictionary of Love. It is an anthology of over 650 quotations on love from the profane to the profound arranged alphabetically into 211 subject categories by over 350 authors.

How to Be Totally Unhappy in a Peaceful World: A Complete Manual with Rules, Exercises, a Midterm and Final Exam.

The Bush Calendar: Four More Years???

Dedications and Acknowledgements

First, I would like to dedicate this book to and thank my late friend, Richard Liebow, for introducing me to the work of Gurdjieff during our walks in San Francisco in the late sixties and early seventies. I would also like to thank him for encouraging me, after I attended several of his weekly meetings in San Francisco, to start a study group in the town I live in. My thanks to two members of my study group, Elaine Weinreb and Cheron O'Brian, who read early drafts of the manuscript and thought the book would be of use and encouraged me to publish it.

I would like to thank the following people who all read the manuscript and made valuable suggestions for improving both its form and helping clarify my ideas as how to present them: Ruth Silverberg, Sharon Rice, Christina Pirruccello, Sue Ann Armstrong, Ramón Stevens, Helen Friedman, Jinny Connolly, Gisela Linder, and Katie Waugh-Kelso. I wish to give a special thanks to Eric Gregory for all his efforts in producing and publishing the final version of this book. I also want to express my sincere thanks to Toby Griggs for helping me to produce revised versions of this book and helping it to become an e-Book. My heartfelt thanks go to all of the above persons. In the end, all the mistakes in grammar, style, or in the content of the ideas discussed in the book are solely my responsibility.

Table of Contents

Introduction

I am totally unqualified to write this book. This, however, is not the first time that I have been totally unqualified to write a book. While teaching Family Law at Warwick University in England, I wrote the book, *How to Conduct Your Own Divorce in England and Wales and a Guide to the Divorce Laws*. There was probably no one in England who had fewer qualifications than I. Yet it was published, received a few good reviews, and went into three editions. I also compiled a book of quotations on love entitled *A Dictionary of Love* that was later republished as *Love Notes: Quotations from the Heart*. Again, I can think of no one who knows less about love than I, but then as one friend said, "Who really knows anything about love?" The only book that I was fully qualified to write was *How to be Totally Unhappy in a Peaceful World: A Complete Manual with Rules, Exercises, a Midterm and Final Exam*. So how can I take up such a serious subject as writing on Gurdjieff and Ouspensky, who was Gurdjieff's primary student and a prolific writer on this subject?

Who This Book was Written For

When a writer sets out to write, if he is a professional, he supposedly knows the target audience the book is for. In fact, real pros in the nonfiction field can write the ad for the book to the specific target market before they write the book. I am writing this book to see if I can lay out some of the basic principles with the hope that by writing them out I can better apply them to my life.

1

Nevertheless, if this book ever gets into anyone else's hands, I hope he or she finds it of some value and worth whatever time spent on it.

However, since I make no claims of being an expert in this field, I warn the reader that I may have omitted key elements of the teachings or I may have incorrectly interpreted some of the concepts. I have followed the premise of Benjamin Disraeli, the nineteenth-century British Prime Minister, who said, "The best way to learn about a subject is to write a book about it." I also thought about Ouspensky's suggestion that sometimes one can understand something one does not understand by trying to explain it to others. Certainly putting the ideas down on paper and trying to explain it to myself gives the ideas a specificity that I could not get by just talking about them. If I knew nothing about a subject, it becomes fairly apparent when I put it down on paper. So by writing this book, I have had to research many of the concepts discussed here. Whether I got it right in the final analysis, for me, will be whether I actually change.

There is one other point I want to make about this teaching. All the concepts in it are interdependent. Therefore, in discussing the ideas of the system, instead of thinking of it as a straight line it is better to think of it as a circle. A person can start anywhere in the system and it will eventually lead to everything in the system, so the concepts that I started with in the beginning could have come later in the book and vice versa. Furthermore, there is a tendency to repeat certain ideas as the book advances. This is because when I start writing about a new idea, it will be related to ones I have already discussed, and to give a complete, or at least a fuller, idea of the new topic, I have to bring in ideas I have already discussed. Perhaps the real reason is that I am just verbose and repetitious. I'll let you be the judge. Even if I am correct in describing the ideas, there is still the danger discussed below.

The Danger of a Straightforward Presentation
of Gurdjieff's Work

There are many concepts in the teachings of Gurdjieff. The concepts come under the general category called the Work. Even if I have rendered the ideas I discuss correctly, there is still a danger in just laying out the ideas of the Work. One of the greatest dangers of the Work is that it can become purely a matter of memory. Then the Work would simply lie in the outer memory and the entire value of the Work would drop to zero. It would be something outside the person and not inside them. It would not be emotional. It would not touch them and—according to Maurice Nicoll, a teacher of the Work—a system of esoteric teaching that always takes itself as final becomes mere memory. Therefore, one could read my book and recite the concepts from it from memory and not have applied any of the ideas but, rather, think that somehow they knew what the Work is about.

The Work has three phases. The first is that we value it. To value it, we must know what the ideas are that it brings forth. If we don't know the ideas of the Work, we can't go on. The second step is actually applying the ideas of the Work to our lives. If we don't apply them to our lives, we have just learned another branch of information that we can keep in our memory and recite like a parrot. It is the second stage where the Work really begins. The third stage of the

Work is to realize how difficult it is to apply these ideas to our lives. It is not something that we can master in a few months or years. It is a lifelong process.

Note to Reader

Although the ideas discussed in this book come from Gurdjieff, I want to make it clear they did not originate with him. He was the transmitter of the ideas. It is the ideas that are of importance, much more so than the man. Since many great men, religious or otherwise, often turn out to have feet of clay because they are also human, we can become disillusioned with them as men and therefore disregard the ideas they were teaching. The ideas in this book have a long history that includes Christ, the Sufis, the Taoists and many other groups whose work was the transformation of man. The idea of true alchemy was not turning lead into gold, but the transformation of ourselves, as anyone can attest to who has tried to change anything in him or herself. Gurdjieff learned many of these ideas from his travels as a young man.

There are many ideas and concepts in this book. The reader is not asked to take any on faith. The reader must understand and verify these ideas and methods in his or her own life, and might find a few ideas useful and the rest useless or even completely incomprehensible. Use what you can use and ignore the rest. Even one idea in this book can make a big difference in your life.

Studies show that only ten percent of the people who start a nonfiction book read beyond the first chapter. I hope you will read on.

I think the ideas in this book will be better received if one comes to it with an open mind. If we think we know everything we are reading already because we are a philosophy professor or successful in some other branch of life, we can be shutting ourselves off from some very important concepts that can have a profound effect on our lives. Do not be like the professor who went to visit the Zen master and kept on talking, not letting the Zen master say anything. The Zen master poured the professor tea and after filling his cup, kept pouring tea, spilling it over the table. When the professor protested, the Zen master said that this cup was like the professor's mind, so full of itself that nothing could enter it. Since the purpose of the teachings in this book is to make us think in a new way, I hope you will leave some space in your mind to allow some of these ideas to enter. Even if many of the ideas seem foreign to you, and even if you subsequently reject them, give these ideas a chance to be heard. Who Gurdjieff and Ouspensky were is discussed next.

Who Were Gurdjieff and Ouspensky?

Georges Ivanovitch Gurdjieff (1872-1949) was born in Alexandropol on the border of Russia and Turkey. He was a Caucasian, a Georgian. In his youth he was a searcher and had many unanswered questions. Just as many youths in the sixties and even today seek the answers in the East, Gurdjieff's early travels to places in Central Asia and the Middle East lasted twenty years. He then settled in Moscow and started forming groups in both Moscow and St. Petersburg at about the time of the First World War to teach his system of ideas and methods. He gathered students and taught in Germany, England and France in the 1920s and 1930s. He chose to remain in Paris all through the German Occupation in the 1940s to go on with his work. The story of Gurdjieff's early life is in his book, *Meetings with Remarkable Men*, which is listed by a panel of fifteen scholars to be one of the hundred best spiritual books of the twentieth century.

Gurdjieff might be thought of as the first major coffeehouse philosopher. He liked to meet people in coffeehouses, the noisier the better. The prospective student had to concentrate very hard over the sound of other conversations and the general noise of the coffeehouse to hear what Gurdjieff was saying. One apparently needed total concentration to follow Gurdjieff. The slightest amount of daydreaming or lapse in attention and all was lost.

Gurdjieff also did much of his writing in coffeehouses. Not only was Gurdjieff a coffeehouse aficionado, but he was very outgoing and loved to hold elaborate dinners that he often, with the help of his students, spent all afternoon preparing. There was plenty of wine and other alcoholic beverages at these dinners and they went on well into the night. Gurdjieff was the total opposite of the quiet philosopher who sits in his study by himself for many hours thinking, reflecting and writing. Gurdjieff apparently loved being around people and, except in his early years, he was always surrounded by and traveled with a large following of students.

Gurdjieff met with Ouspensky and other students during World War I and the Russian revolution; due to the chaotic conditions, the group moved to Essentuki in the Caucasus, and then through Tiflis, Constantinople, Berlin, and London. In London, Gurdjieff and Ouspensky split for the last time. Gurdjieff went to the Chateau du Priecuré near Paris, where he opened the Institute for the Harmonious Development of Man in 1922. Many of his students wrote books about their experiences with Gurdjieff and the ideas of the system.

In 1924 Gurdjieff visited America. He was one of the great philosophers on esotericism. He was also apparently reckless behind the wheel of an automobile and had a serious accident on one of the highways surrounding Manhattan. He went back to Paris, where he concentrated on writing and working with his students. He died in 1949.

Gurdjieff's main writings include: *Beelzebub's Tales to His Grandson: An Objectively Impartial Criticism of the Life of Man; Meetings with Remarkable Men; Life is Real Only Then, When "I Am";* and *Views from the Real World: Early Talks of Gurdjieff.*

P.D. Ouspensky (1878-1947) was born in Russia. He was a professional journalist, but extremely interested in esotericism. In 1907, at age 29, Ouspensky traveled to Constantinople, Smyrna, Greece, and Egypt. He wrote a few books, including *Tertium Organum*, and gave public lectures on Yoga, the Tarot, Superman and on other esoteric subjects. He then decided to go to the East to search for the miraculous and in 1913 and 1914 traveled to Egypt, Ceylon and India. Not finding what he was looking for in India, he came back to Moscow. There was a small ad in a newspaper that attracted him; it was about a meeting where dance movements of a magical nature were to take place. It was there that he met Gurdjieff. In 1915, he started studying with Gurdjieff but made one condition. Ouspensky told Gurdjieff that he was a writer and he would not study with Gurdjieff unless he could write about his experience. Gurdjieff agreed, and the result was Ouspensky's book, *In Search of the Miraculous: Fragments of an Unknown Teaching*. More than two thirds of the book is Ouspensky quoting Gurdjieff. The book was published posthumously. Ouspensky died in 1947 and the manuscript was sent to Gurdjieff who authorized its publication and it was published in 1949. The same panel of fifteen scholars who included Gurdjieff's *Meetings With Remarkable Men* as one of the hundred best spiritual books of the twentieth century. also included Ouspensky's *In Search of the Miraculous* in this esteemed list.

Ouspensky studied with Gurdjieff for approximately eight years until they had their final split in January 1923. Ouspensky continued teaching his own group that was centered in England where he had started teaching in 1921. Ouspensky spent the last seven years of his life, from 1941 to 1947, in New York City where his book, *The Psychology of Man's Possible Evolution*, was written. It consisted of five lectures that were read by Ouspensky's students to groups interested in the Work. In March 1947 Ouspensky returned to England and died there a few months later.

Maurice Nicoll (1884-1953), a psychoanalyst and student of Jung, was one of Ouspensky's students. Nicoll met Ouspensky in 1921. Nicoll spent the following year in France studying with Gurdjieff. In

1931, Ouspensky requested that Nicoll initiate a program to pass on the ideas he learned. I mainly relied on Nicoll's work to write this book.

This Primer Does Not Cover the Entire Teachings

There are many concepts in the teachings of Gurdjieff .These concepts are all positive, have many levels of complexity, and are multidimensional in meaning, from the obvious to the subtle. Far be it from me to think that I can explain them all. Some, if not many, I do not as yet understand, and perhaps never will. Ouspensky's subtitle to his classic book, *In Search of the Miraculous* is *Fragments of an Unknown Teaching*. If Ouspensky could give only fragments of the teaching, it would be very presumptuous of me to think I could lay out the complete system in this simple primer.

What Is the Purpose of the Work?

The purpose of the Work is nothing short of transforming ourselves into different people. By applying the principles laid down in the Work, we should be able to change. Therefore, it is very different from just learning a new subject. For example, if we learn Spanish, we are the same person we were before, but now, in a manner of speaking, we have added talking, writing and reading Spanish to our repertoire of skills. We have not changed our being one iota. We have changed our level of knowledge. This Work is about changing our level of being. It is the true alchemy, not changing lead into gold, but transforming ourselves into higher beings. There are many, which at present include me, who have read many books by Gurdjieff, Ouspensky and many of their students, but have not changed their level of being much, if at all. They know the Work or parts of it, as someone might know a foreign language. To Gurdjieff this is a total misuse or waste of the Work. Unless we apply the principles to ourselves and start changing, we are just engaging in an intellectual exercise, which might be okay to the student of the Work if he just wants to add another intellectual game to his bag of tricks, but it is not what the Work is about.

The Difference Between Knowledge and Being

We can all agree that there are different levels of knowledge and skills. We can easily see that the person who learns a subject, be it Spanish or playing the violin, has acquired knowledge of the subject or acquired a skill. If we have studied Spanish for five years and traveled to Spanish speaking countries, we obviously would have more knowledge of Spanish than if we had never studied it or just studied Spanish for a short time. We would also think it reasonable that for us to learn Spanish well, it would take many years. It is not something that can be accomplished in a short time.

We all can assume that some people are more knowledgeable or skillful in the various fields they have studied and practiced in. When it comes to our beings, the general consensus seems to be that we are all human beings and one human being isn't better or higher than the next. We are all basically the same. Occasionally, we read about some outstanding person such as

Mother Teresa, Mahatma Gandhi, or any of the other religious leaders the world has produced, whether they be Jesus Christ, Mohammed, or Buddha, and think these people were different. They had a unique quality about their being and were different from us.

Unfortunately, today many so called "religious leaders" or persons in the new age movement who have written many books turn out, themselves, to have feet of clay. They have done things in the end that make us lose respect for them, such as run away with one of their disciples' wives, or had been promiscuous, or lived like kings off the sweat of their followers, and so we think these people are basically just like everyone else, or worse! Occasionally, though, we do come across people who act differently. They take the ups and downs of life in a steadier manner than we do. They are more even-tempered. They have a certain quality that does impress us. Nothing seems to drive them off their base. They seem more balanced and at ease despite what has happened to them in the world. These people can be thought of as having a higher level of being than we have. These people occur at all levels of income, social status, race, nationality.

Where Do We Live?

If we were asked where we live, we would give a city, and if asked more specifically we could give an address within the city and could describe the physical aspects of our home, apartment, house, how large, how many rooms and so on. That is where we live

11

physically. The crucial question in terms of the Work is where we live psychologically. The space within our head is much larger than any particular physical home. It has many rooms and whole neighborhoods. Where do we hang out in our psychological world? Are we in a good psychological space or a bad one? There are some neighborhoods within our psychological world that are just plain dangerous, such as neighborhoods in the physical world where we wouldn't want to take a walk at night by ourselves. We are in a terrible mood in these places and we can get into all sorts of trouble if we stay there long enough or sometimes even for a brief period. We have all met people who are constantly angry. What kind of place are they in their interior world? This interior place reflects the level of our being.

When we ask someone what they have done today or the last few days, the response is a chronological list of what they have done in linear time, never where they have been in their interior. And in a sense people do not want to know where we have been internally. All we can really say is, "I feel good," or "I feel bad," but no one really wants a litany of reasons why we feel bad. People ask, How are things going? as a polite way of making conversation. They don't want to listen to a whole list of physical ailments and problems.

So, in a sense, time swamps our being. We have a past, a brief present and a future, and they all consist of a chronology of things we have done, are doing, or plan to do. They can be seen as a horizontal line where the left part is our past and the right side is our plan for the future. While the chronological list of what we are doing over time stands in the foreground, our being remains in the background. This hides the importance of our being and what level of being we are on. We could think of our being as a vertical line that intersects the horizontal line, like a cross. This system, without going into much detail is a form of Christian esotericism. The Gospels, and particularly Christ's words and parables, are studied for their hidden meanings that deal with the psychological transformation of man. Our place on this vertical line, which represents being, rises up or down according to the level of being one is on, reflecting how we view what happens to us on the every day horizontal line. These levels, which might be thought of as parallel wires that do not touch, represent different levels of being. The higher the level of being, the closer we come to the Higher Powers or God. On a very practical level, the importance of our level of being is that our level of being attracts our life and everything in it.

Our Level of Being Attracts Our Life

A very simple way to find out what level of being we are presently on is to look at our life and see what is happening there. What kind of people are we dealing with? Are they pleasant, easy to get along with, or very argumentative and hostile? Our level of being attracts everything that happens to us. This is independent of all social and economic conditions. There are millionaires who are total grumps and utterly unpleasant to be around, and waitresses who are a complete pleasure to be around. There are also, of course, millionaires who are very pleasant and waitresses who are grumps."

As the Chinese proverb goes, "Until age forty a man has the face he was born with, at forty he has the face he deserves." George

Orwell was a bit more patient, and said, "At age fifty every man has the face he deserves." Our face reflects our level of being as we mature. Everyone makes us happy, some when they come and some when they go. When do we make people happy? There is no way we can change our circumstances to affect what we attract unless we make a change in our level of being. As the long-forgotten poet Samuel Hoffenstein observed, "Wherever I go, I go too, and spoil everything." Or as the story or perhaps fable goes, a man was moving to a new town and he met an old-timer there and asked him how the people were in the new town. The old-timer returned the question and asked, "How were people in the town you came from?" The newcomer replied that they were pretty unfriendly and argumentative. The old-timer replied, "I'm afraid that's what the people in this town are like." Another newcomer to the town met the same old-timer, asked the same question, and after the old-timer responded with his same question, the newcomer replied, "They were friendly, helpful people." The old-timer informed him, as you have no doubt guessed, that the people in this town were friendly and helpful.

One way to look at our being is that our being projects a sphere around us. This sphere might be somewhat analogous to the concept that everyone has an aura around them. This sphere is what allows certain things into our sphere and prevents other things from entering our lives. If one could see it physically, it might have a bulge in one place or a dent in another. As long as this sphere remains the same, our lives remain the same. There are some who go away to a monastery to try to radically change what events can come to them. This way may work for some.

The Work's solution is that by taking in new knowledge, and then by self-observation, we can see our being and the shape of the sphere we have created around ourselves. The Work says we can never really change by what others tell us to do; we must see for ourselves what needs changing. This is why advice is so useless, although most of us can't avoid giving it on occasion. If we give advice and it is successful, we are resented; if the advice fails, we are blamed. So the crucial question is how do we go about changing our level of being? Changing our circumstances is a total waste of time. In the words of the English writer Samuel Johnson, "The fountain of content must spring up in the mind, and he who has so little knowledge of human nature as to seek happiness by changing anything but his own disposition will waste his life in fruitless efforts and multiply the grief he proposed to remove."

There are two basic questions that arise from this premise that are worth exploring: first, why don't people accept this idea? According to the Work, there are three illusions that keep us from believing that our level of being attracts our life. The first illusion is that if something happens to us that we don't like we do not accept responsibility for it but, rather, blame others or circumstances for what happened. It is not our fault. Of course, if things happen that we do like, we are perfectly willing to accept the fact that our being caused it. In short, we get the A's and B's of life while others give us the C's, D's, and God forbid, F's. Therefore, we do not believe our level of being attracts bad things in our life. Other people or circumstances are at

15

fault, not us.

The second illusion is that we think we know ourselves. If we could really see how we behave, we would be shocked. Remember the first time we heard our recorded voice? We were probably surprised, and not pleasantly, at how it sounded. If we could see how we act, the same thing would happen. We are probably much better judges of how others act than of ourselves. The Work gives many reasons why we don't know ourselves, which will be discussed later. For now, the main point is that since we are under the illusion that we know ourselves, we refuse to believe that our level of being causes unpleasant things to happen to us.

The third illusion that prevents us from believing that our level of being attracts our life is the illusion that things will get better over time; that things will change favorably for us without our doing anything to make them better. The truth is that as we get older, things get worse, not better. We start to crystallize and become fixed in our patterns, which makes change that much more difficult. This is why as we get older we become more difficult to live with. We have these patterns, or rigid edges, that rub against others in wrong ways and because these patterns are fixed, they are extremely difficult to change or even adapt a bit to other people's patterns. Nothing will change unless we change our level of being.

Is our level of being fixed at one point or is it on a continuum? Let us assume that our level of being goes from number 1, a terrible person such as Hitler, to 100 a godlike or perfect person. If someone were a 25 how could he or she change? They would be fixed there for

16

life. The reality is that everyone occupies a continuum in the level of being, say for example, from 20 to 30. Therefore, our being has some degree of freedom. We all know that some days are much better than others for us, and sometimes as we say, we get out of bed on the wrong side and everything that day goes wrong. If we are on the upper continuum of our level of being we will attract better things in our life. We could be "on a roll." So the trick is to live our lives on the upper side of our scale. If we do that then perhaps, for example, the scale of our level of being might rise from 25 to 35. Of course, our level of being could also go in the downward direction if we are always living on the bottom of our scale of being

The big question is how can we change our level of being? That is what the Work is about and what this book is about. To give us a glimpse of the answer, the only way we can change our level of being is to change the way we react to what is happening in our life. The Work says that if we keep reacting the same way to external events in our life, our level of being remains the same. *Only by reacting differently* can we change our level of being and then attract different things in our life than we are presently attracting. And our level of being also determines what we consider good and bad in our life.

The Good, the Bad, and the Purpose of the Work

The reality is that no one acts with evil intentions. Everyone acts for what he or she thinks is good. What we think is good, however, depends on our level of being. To a person whose level of being makes him or her a criminal, to steal is good. He doesn't see himself as bad. Someone once asked Willie Sutton, a notorious bank robber, why he kept robbing banks. He replied, "Because that's where the money is." Nothing personal. He had no bad intentions. All the people who, during Prohibition, broke the law by supplying alcohol to the public, didn't consider that what they were doing was wrong. They were just giving the public what they wanted: alcohol. The present growers of marijuana feel exactly the same way. They are giving people what they want.

We have all experienced what we once thought of as being good as no longer being good. Perhaps at one time in our lives we thought that going to bars and getting loaded was a great way to spend an evening, but now we no longer think this is a very good idea. As we go up the continuum, our behavior will change. Perhaps at one time in our lives we thought that if we were angry it was good to "let it all hang out", go into a rage and be violent either physically or verbally to the people around us. Perhaps, later as we our level of being changed, we no longer thought it is a good idea but, rather, struggle to control the expression of our negative emotions. Perhaps, we have learned that expressing negative emotions rather than offering a release just leads to more negative emotions.

Understanding Each Other and Our Level of Being

One of the Work concepts involving the premise that our level of being attracts our life is that we cannot understand someone who is above our own level of being. On the knowledge side this idea seems easy enough to accept. For example, if someone has a Ph.D. in physics and is discussing the intricacies of quantum mechanics, it would be easy to accept the fact that the average person would not understand what was being talked about. Well, the Work states that the same applies to a person's level of being. Perhaps the reason that Jesus was not understood by most people in His time or, for that matter, people of our time who now read His words and parables in the Bible, is because Jesus was on a much higher level of being than the vast majority of people.

In the twentieth century, it may be why so many people did not understand the power of Gandhi's nonviolence movement. With no weapons or arms of any kind, he was able to rid India of the British, who had been their colonial oppressors for hundreds of years. The British were totally nonplussed by Gandhi's tactics of nonviolence, which commenced with his long march to the sea in protest against the salt tax the British had imposed on the Indian population.

In America, the nonviolent tactics of Martin Luther King, Jr., and the nonviolent sit-ins and peaceful boycotts were not understood by the political powers of the South. King and his followers had a higher level of being than the political powers and much of the population of the South as well as the North. This brings up the question of what exactly is good and bad.

Good and Bad and the Concept of Aim

While we are discussing good and bad, I would like to discuss the Work's concept of the relativity of good and bad. We all know as

19

discussed earlier that some things we once thought of as good we now think of as bad. We all know that some practices that are considered good in some cultures are considered bad in others. The Work says that what is good and bad can be understood only if we see them in relation to a third factor, which is aim. Let us suppose two cars are driving north from New York City on a highway that goes to Boston. One car's destination is Boston. Obviously, the driver is doing the right thing. In the other car, the driver's destination is Washington, D.C. Equally obvious, he is going in the wrong direction and his behavior is bad in relation to his aim. Without an aim, it would not be possible to decide if either driver was right or wrong. One of the Work's aims is to raise our level of being. Therefore, anything that tends to raise our level of being is good and anything that tends to lower our level of being is bad.

So What Is the Work About and How Is It Different?

The Work is about changing our level of being. This is the work of all systems of transformation. The goal is the same. The difference, as I see it, is in the methods used, some of which I believe are unique, that give more handles to help us in this arduous task of changing our being. The Work is definitely not for everyone. In fact, very few who take up the spiritual trip ever find it, and of those who find it, relatively few stick with it. It is not an easy path. It makes certain assumptions about life.

Some of the Work's Assumptions—The Concept of Progress

Gurdjieff made very clear that he did not think that mankind is progressing. It is true that technically we have all sorts of inventions that are supposed to make our lives better, but, as Henry David Thoreau asked, "Do we ride on the railroad or does the railroad ride on us?" These technological wonders were supposed to free us from the drudgery of work, and the computer was going to eliminate the need for paper. It seems that the more technology we have, the more man has been enslaved by it, and we work harder and spend more time taking care of our numerous possessions. According to one study, Americans in 1999 worked 143 hours more a year than they worked in 1970. That is an increase of three-and-a-half weeks of work a year. Is this progress? Is modern man any happier or wiser than the caveman was? I doubt it.

Moreover, has man really progressed over the ages, or has he actually deteriorated? According to ancient teachings, man originally lived in a golden age, then in a silver age, then brass and finally in an iron age. The Hindus claim that the age we are living in now—the Kali age—is the age that is man's lowest point of evolution. The names of the ages are not important, but the idea is that man has progressively degenerated rather than progressively evolved. The Work claims that man in the past was in better circumstances, despite all our technology, and in a far better inner state than he is today.

The Work states that it is a very naïve belief that the passage of time automatically brings progress and that one must get rid of that notion. When people get older, do they necessarily become wiser or better? Is the newest fashion necessarily better than the older one? Is tomorrow necessarily going to be better than today? Progress implies that our children will always live better than we do. The son or daughter should outperform their father and mother: Life should always be an upward spiral, usually involving more possessions, power and prestige.

As to the emotions that man experiences, have they changed at all? What the poet Homer said thousands of years ago, or what Shakespeare wrote, is just as true today because people are basically the same.

Of course, the main argument for progress is the increase of longevity. The caveman supposedly lived to a ripe old age of eighteen or so, whereas we have life expectancies into the seventies and longer. H. Leighton Steward, Morrison Beatha, M.D., Sam S. Andrews, M.D., and Luis A. Balart, M.D., in their book *Sugar Busters*, point out some information on average life span that might surprise you. They state that while the statistic that man's life has increased by 50 percent in the last century is accurate, it is nearly all due to a tremendous decrease in infant and early childhood mortality. For middle-aged American men (+/-50 years old), they live only eighteen months longer than they did in 1900. This proves true, the authors point out, despite the availability of flu shots, penicillin for pneumonia, antibiotics, among other advances and breakthroughs of modern medicine.

Others claim that what the above authors say may be true for the first half of the 20th century, but that in the second half of the century substantial gains were made on increasing longevity that were not dependent on cutting infant and childhood mortality. Even if this were the case, it is also true that we are currently experiencing epidemics of diabetes, cancer, hypertension, heart disease, obesity and, as the frosting on our epidemic cake, we have a growing epidemic of senility, including Alzheimer's disease, in our older population. So although some people live very well into old age, many have illnesses that totally incapacitate them. During the last twelve years of life, most Americans can no longer take care of themselves. Although civilization as a whole has not progressed, it is possible for the single individual man or woman to progress.

The Work Assumption of Individual Effort

The Work assumes that an individual can develop himself. The Work assumes we are all born incomplete and that whereas the first birth is physical, the second birth is the development of our being. Two steps accomplish this. The first is taking in new knowledge so that we are able to think in new ways, and then applying that new knowledge to ourselves. If we just take in the knowledge by reading books, attending lectures or workshops, and filling notebooks with what was being said, we are in the same situation as someone learning a subject that he doesn't apply, and it is useless. We need the new knowledge, but it must be applied to our lives.

This is a requirement that all esoteric teachings demand. We, ourselves, are actually the only ones who can make the effort. We can get guidance from a teacher, or a book, but we have to make the effort or it is just a useless exercise that we will eventually tire of. We must value the new information and then apply it. We must make a conscious effort. Nothing can be transformed mechanically by some automatic method wherein we hear the ideas and somehow by some mechanical osmotic process, we change. This is a process that takes a long time. It should not be thought that we can hear the new ideas in a weekend workshop and then we will have lasting change. We will already start to come down from the high we had at the workshop as we drive away.

The process of change was well described by the American psychoanalyst Allen Wheelis in his 1973 book *How People Change*, in which he discusses the following sequence for change: 1. Personality change follows change in behavior, and since we are what we do, if we want to change what we are, we must begin by changing what we do. We must undertake a new mode of action; 2. Since the significance of such action is change, this new mode of action will run into much resistance because the existing entrenched forces will protest and resist; 3. The new behavior will be experienced as difficult, unnatural and anxiety provoking because it is outside our comfort zone; 4. Although the new mode of behavior may be undertaken lightly, it can be sustained only by considerable effort or will; 5. Change will occur only if such new behavior is maintained over a sufficiently long period of time.

The main point I want to bring up here is that considerable effort is required to change and only over a long period of time. The new age idea that we either do it or don't do it, and that trying is some form of resistance, is absurd. It would be like telling a toddler that he should just start walking and stop his fooling around and continually falling down. The reason why all toddlers finally do learn to walk is that after falling down a couple of thousand times they finally learn the skill of standing and walking steadily. So in any work on ourselves where we are trying to change, we must realize we must take tiny baby steps and may fail many times before we finally master any change, and only then can we move on to slightly bigger challenges. We should not be critical of ourselves for falling down many times. The important thing is to keep getting up and to keep trying.

An excellent poem by Portia Nelson describing this process is entitled "Autobiography in Five Short Chapters" and appears in her book, *There's a Hole in My Sidewalk: The Romance of Self Discovery* (Atria Books/Beyond Words, 1994). It shows the difficulties in making any change. It reads as follows:

1) I walk down the street.

There is a deep hole in the sidewalk.

I fall in.

I am lost . . . I am hopeless.

It isn't my fault.

It takes forever to find a way out.

2) I walk down the same street.

There is a deep hole in the sidewalk.

I pretend I don't see it.

I fall in again.

I can't believe I am in the same place.

But, it isn't my fault.

It takes a long time to get out.

3) I walk down the same street.

There is a deep hole in the sidewalk.

I see it is there.

I still fall in . . . it's a habit.

My eyes are open.

I know where I am.

It is my fault.

I get out immediately.

4) I walk down the same street.

There is a deep hole in the sidewalk.

I walk around it.

5) I walk down another street.

Whereas Dr. Wheelis talks about making changes in personality, the Work talks about changes in our very being, the essence of ourselves, which will be spoken about later on. For now the key point is that only by conscious effort can any change be made, and that effort must be done by us. The Work says we must have the will to work, and that the will starts with affection. Unless we value the Work emotionally, we will not attempt to apply it. The phrase used in the Work is to "catch the rope overhead," and we will not reach for it unless we realize the danger we are in. The rope, in fact, is the Work and lies just above us but at a higher level. We can catch the rope only by making conscious efforts and then the Work will be effective for us. The Work starts to teach us in those moments when we are not identified with our various problems, in periods of silence, and in those gaps in our mechanical lives where ordinarily everything is a blank, or we are bored.

The Work Assumption
Life Does Not Become Easy After Studying the Work

Another assumption that the Work makes is that even if we develop ourselves and raise our level of being, there will never be a point in our lives where we won't have to face life's problems or, as some like to call them, challenges. What the Work offers, in addition to any esoteric system for inner change, is that the system learned becomes something between us and life, a screen by which we take in life events and have a better way of dealing with them. If we have no inner philosophy or system, we will be swamped by life's events. There is always something happening to us or in the world that can throw us off balance and totally upset us. The Work gives a series of specific concepts which if applied by conscious effort, will enable us to not be swamped by life's events.

Who Can Study the Work? Good Householders—Yes;
Tramps, Lunatics, and Hasnamous—No

The Work says that no one can benefit from it unless he or she has arrived at the level of the Good Householder. By Good

Householder, it is meant that someone has made it in life. They have a successful career and can support themselves and others. They have made the ordinary efforts to establish themselves in the world. They can do at least one thing well. Gurdjieff used to say if you can show me a man who can do anything well, such as make a good cup of coffee with all that implies, I can teach him other things.

The second requirement is that the Good Householder who is attracted to the Work, although he is part of life, does not believe in life and does not believe that life leads anywhere. He views life differently. He realizes that no matter what he does in life, it will never solve his problems and he has developed a Magnetic Center. The Good Householder who believes in life but has not developed a Magnetic Center believes that life will answer his problems and, therefore, makes no attempt to look other than in the material world for the answer to his problems.

The Work says that those who have not made it in this world will not benefit from the Work. It is not a system for people who have failed in life to take up as an escape from life. The Work refers to these people as "tramps." Tramps have no feelings of responsibility toward anything. The Work claims that among tramps there are many artists and poets who despise and look down on Good Householders.

Lunatics, from the Work's perspective, are people who think they can change the world, or at least aspects of it. They are like politicians who have big plans about how they are going to change things without taking into consideration all the resistances (the Second Force, which will be discussed later) they will have to overcome to reach their goals. Often they create greater disorder by their plans and proclamations than before because they did not calculate the resistance involved in reaching their goals. Tramps, Lunatics, and the rest of us all have one thing in common. We all have a fool in us who to a lesser or greater extent fails to take into account the resistances we must overcome to reach our goals.

Hasnamous is a word invented by Gurdjieff from some Persian or Turkish language. According to Gurdjieff, a Hasnamous is a man who is clever enough to see that he can gain power by means of deception over ordinary people. According to Ouspensky, Hasnamous men are people whose well-being depends on the non-well-being of others. Certainly men like Hitler and Stalin, as well as many other dictators, could be thought to be Hasnamous. On the other hand, in ordinary life there have always been people who made their well-being dependent on the ill-being of others. According to the Work, Tramps, Lunatics, and Hasnamous are either not eligible to do, or not capable of doing, the Work. No matter who we are we all come under influences.

The Magnetic Center and A, B, and C Influences

Although there are depths of meanings to all Work concepts, the main idea of a Magnetic Center is that a person with a Center recognizes influences outside of life—that there is something else for him to do aside from what he has already done.

The Work says there are three kinds of influences, called A, B, and C. All A influences come from life. They are the influences that

29

make us get along in the material world, whether it is to make money, build a career, establish a relationship, have a family, or gain fame and fortune for ourselves. They keep us tied to the material world. We think we are progressing under A influences, but it is really like a hall of distorted mirrors where we think that by looking at the mirrors, we are going straight ahead when, in fact, we are going around in circles but never realize it. The influences of A have no connection with B or C influences, and their main function is to keep us asleep. For an extreme example of an A influence, think of a man in a crowd where he adopts the crowd's position and is so influenced that any independent thought or independence from the crowd virtually disappears, and he becomes part of the mass phenomena. Emil Zola's novel *Germinal* gives excellent descriptions of this crowd psychology. We can also read about it in the newspaper how the English soccer fans react with violence. In Brazil they built a moat around one field to keep the crowd from going onto the field and engaging in destructive behavior.

The C influences, at the other extreme, are influences that come directly from enlightened masters, such as Christ, Buddha, and Mohammed. The key point is that the only way we can get C influences is orally from the master Himself. It is a direct transmission without any intermediary coming between the master and the listener.

The B influences are the teachings of the enlightened masters coming to us through intermediary sources. For example, Christ's parables in the New Testament are examples of B teachings because we read about them; in fact, the men who wrote them, such as Paul, never actually heard Christ speak. Those who actually heard Christ speak were getting C influences. The same goes for Buddha. Those who heard him received C influences. His students, who wrote about the Buddha and his teachings—sometimes hundreds of years after Buddha's death—are giving us B influences. In the nineteenth century, Ramakrishna, a holy man in India whose teaching founded the Vedanta movement, was an enlightened person. The students that he actually taught, such as Swami Vivekananda, were receiving C influences. Through Swami Vivekananda's books, we are receiving B influences.

The important point to remember is that B influences are not influences from life, but from higher sources, and if a man has a Magnetic Center, he can, to a certain extent, distinguish between A and B influences. He starts to come under the influence of some of these B influences. C influences come from even higher sources, and man can only learn about them through B influences, unless he can actually hear an enlightened master himself. The average person does not have access to C influences.

The point the Work makes is that we are all under some influence. All we can do is choose which influence we will be under. For someone without a Magnetic Center, the only influences he follows are A influences. Moreover, he will not even recognize B influences if he is brought in contact with them. If a B influence were pointed out as being something out of the ordinary, he would probably disparage it in some way. If he were in the presence of Jesus, all he would see is a long haired hippie. He is simply not interested in any influences outside of life that his senses cannot take in.

Having a Magnetic Center also means we believe there is something more to life than what our senses can see, hear, taste, and smell. If we believe that what we see is all there is, or what the newspaper reports is real, we would never be interested in any other type of life. We would not think there are those who might guide us to a new, different, higher level of reality, so we would never look. Those who are attracted to the Work (or any esoteric teaching) believe there are higher powers, or God, or any other name we want to choose, and this world may, in fact, be more important and offer more than what they are presently experiencing in their lives.

By doing the Work—or, for that matter, in any esoteric system—in a sense we are "creating ourselves." It is not that we are adding something to ourselves, but that we are discovering what is there already. Just as within an acorn lays a potential giant oak tree, so within any seed there is a plant that can develop. If the seed had no future, that is, could not develop, what would its purpose be? In terms of esotericism, we are all seeds who have the ability to develop ourselves. This is the heart of the Work or, for that matter, any other esoteric system.

How the Work Views Man
1: Multiple Personalities and Lack of Unity

According to the Work, the main characteristic of man is his lack of unity. Instead of being one personality in a body, man has many different 'I's, each 'I' thinking he is the whole person. In a movie that came out years ago, *The Three Faces of Eve*, a woman was portrayed who had multiple personalities, each distinct from the other. The Work claims that this is the story with all of us. As Gurdjieff used to say, the person who sets the alarm clock is different from the person who hears it in the morning. That is why it is so hard to keep on any path or work towards any goal. Each individual 'I' claims to be the whole person, and each 'I' has his own will of what he wants; each 'I' claims he is Friedman, Johnson, or Smith—so Friedman is writing this, not the Real 'I'. The Real 'I' is our true essence and will be discussed in more detail later. As long as he believes that what Friedman does is his Real 'I', he can get and does get in trouble. Friedman can do something such as write a check or make some other type of decision that the rest of his 'I's might have to pay for his entire life.

This multiplicity of 'I's and our lack of unity should make us very leery of thinking that the 'I' in momentary control is the real us. We know we have different personalities in different situations. We might have different personalities when we are at work, at home, with our children, with our friends, with our pets.

Our various 'I's also come in different ages, dress differently, and have different personalities. When we hear someone say to another, usually an adult, to "act your age," the person addressed may literally have acted like the small child he or she was, having actually still retained that small child personality along with all the other ones. Moreover, we not only have many different 'I's, but we also have clusters of these 'I's in different areas of our life. Some of these

33

clusters of 'I's are very dangerous because they make us do things or stay in states that make us very negative. Other clusters of 'I's can make us feel good about ourselves. When each 'I' is in charge, he thinks he is the only 'I' there is and that he is, in fact, Friedman.

The analogy often used in the Work is that there is a house with various servants and no one is in charge. All of the servants do what they want to do regardless of the consequences they may cause the other 'I's. Each believes he is the only 'I'. If we phoned this house, depending on which servant picked up the phone, we will get a different reply and each would speak authoritatively as if he were Friedman and there were no other 'I's. If we called another time and another servant answered the phone, we would get a different 'I' representing Friedman, so we might easily get a response that is contradictory from what we heard the last time we called. The voice would be the same, but another personality or 'I' would be in charge. For Friedman himself does not have a Deputy Steward, as the Work calls him, directing the various 'I's to act appropriately.

Each 'I' does what it wants to do when it is in charge and this leads to a life of confusion and conflict. The 'I' that wants to go on a diet is different from the 'I' that stands in front of the refrigerator late at night and can't wait to open the door to see "what's good to eat." Therefore, one of the purposes of the Work is to bring the various 'I's under the direction of the Deputy Steward. Then life can go smoothly toward reaching goals and no one 'I' can cause trouble by acting when it is not appropriate and make the person pay a very big price for the action of this one 'I'. This is referred to as bringing unity or balance to man.

There is one other point I would like to make about our various 'I's in connection with what we allow ourselves to be influenced by. Earlier we discussed allowing ourselves to be under either A or B influences. We can allow ourselves to come under the influence of various 'I' or groupings of 'I's. For example, we can allow ourselves to come under the influence of those 'I's in us that are very critical and then move around in a critical mode, or we can allow ourselves to come under the influence of those 'I's who make us ill. Elizabeth Taylor once commented that she got colds from listening to weather reports. Allowing ourselves to come under the influence of the wrong group of 'I's can make us continually unhappy. Just as we would not want to stay in a bad neighborhood in the external world, so we have to guard ourselves from being under the influence of our negative 'I's. The question arises as to why we can't see our various 'I's." The answer is because of "buffers."

The Concept of Buffers

If man has multiple personalities, why doesn't he see them? The Work says that if man saw all his various personalities and their contradictions, he would go mad. Therefore, to prevent man from seeing his contradictions, he has buffers within himself that prevent him from seeing these contradictions. The Work uses the analogy of the shock absorbers between railroad cars that help cushion the shock when the various separate railroad cars bump against each other. They soften the blow. Buffers prevent man from going insane from all his internal contradictions. When we look at other people it is relatively easy to see their contradictions, but buffers prevent us from seeing our own.

Part of the Work is to see our contradictions on both sides of the buffer at the same time, so the buffer can be brought down. This can be done only by conscious effort and it affects our consciousness. Let us say, for example, that we have the picture of ourselves that we are honest and a situation arises in which we see we are not honest. For example, suppose we are in a checkout line and we see the clerk ring up the wrong price for an item we are buying and that price favors us. All we have to do is say nothing and we will have gained a few cents or dollars. We say nothing, and as we leave the store we realize we are not quite as honest as we thought we were. Here we are able to see the contradiction between our picture of ourselves as being honest and our actual behavior. To see this contradiction is to raise our consciousness to see both sides of the buffer at the same time.

Buffers not only stop or keep us from seeing who we really are, but also who other people are. They also keep us asleep to all signs and portents. Often this places us in danger. For example, a girlfriend and I were once on a hike in the mountains and intent on reaching the peak. The skies suddenly clouded up as they do over mountains. Yet because of our determination to reach the peak, we did not pay attention to these clouds. We even saw the marmots stand on their hind legs and whistle their alarm as they usually do before a big storm, but we were determined to reach the peak. Instead of stopping, we were blinded by our buffers, and proceeded. In a little while, the rain started and we got soaked. On the way down it began to hail. Buffers prevented us from heeding the obvious signs that we should have turned back. We felt lucky to be able to get down from the mountain without any injuries. The 'I' that was determined to reach the peak was different from the sensible 'I' who wanted to preserve my life from danger.

More often, buffers do not place us in danger, but prevent us from truly appreciating life, nature, animals, and people. For example, we can get so tied up in our careers and earning money that our children grow up before our eyes and we don't participate in or experience their growth. We are too busy to attend their games or school plays. We don't have time to just hang out with them. Then one day we realize that they are almost grown up and about to leave home.

Buffers also keep us from accessing B influences for ourselves. Buffers also keep us from true emotion. Ouspensky says the definition of man is a "lying animal." Buffers are internal lies that come between our Real 'I' and everything outside of us.

Not only do individuals have buffers, but corporations and countries have them as well. For example, a corporation can have making profits its only goal. In the short run, it lays off some of its employees to increase its short-term profits. The buffer prevents the corporation from seeing that these laid off employees are the keys to long-term productivity and profit. In the long run, the company will suffer from this short-term view. A nation can have a buffer that prevents it from seeing how it acts at home with its own people is quite different from the policies and dictators it supports in other countries. These other countries may not believe in the same principles the nation believes in, such as freedom of speech, freedom of the press, and so on.

How the Work Views Man
2: Man Cannot Do, Everything Happens

If the concept of multiple personalities seemed far-fetched, this one will seem even more far out. Everything ordinary we do is mechanical. Our lives are like a machine. We respond to stimuli in a mechanical way. To the great philosopher Spinoza, who was not a teacher of this Work but has many ideas that are in agreement with it, all we do is predetermined and could not have happened in any other way. To Spinoza, a man thinking he could have changed things is like a rock flying through space deciding it can come down and land whenever it wants to. The reason the Work agrees with Spinoza is that it claims man, as a machine, cannot do anything other than what he does. It does not matter whether we read books, or write books; it is all done mechanically and, despite our belief that we can do, we are under an illusion.

Although the Work says man cannot do in any large sense of this term because he is a multiplicity of 'I's with no permanent 'I,' the Work does say man has a small degree of will. Nicoll compares this to the freedom of a violin to move within its case. This small degree of will is what allows man to go in different directions. He can read a book or read the newspaper. He can decide to go to a meeting or class or sit home and watch TV. The small degree of will he has sets the momentum for any change that is possible. If he never uses the will he does have, he can never develop the larger will necessary to see he is really a machine and make any significant internal change.

According to the Work, in a strict sense, to do, means to be able to change. It means to react differently, more consciously and less mechanically. If what we do is always the same, whether it is going through the same routines or writing books, we are not able to change because we are always reacting the same way to external situations.

The only way we can realize we are machines is to observe ourselves and see that we react the same way over and over to external events. If we do not try to justify our repetitive reactions, we will observe that we really do act like machines. Of course, no one wants to be a machine so this is a big motivation in the Work to change. In fact, the Work defines intelligence as the "power of adaptation." The extent to which we always react in the same way to external events is a measure of our lack of intelligence. This brings up the next issue: Why do we always react in the same way to external events?

Why Can't Man Do? Because He Is Asleep

One of the main ideas of the Work is that man is asleep. The Bible keeps telling us to awaken, but if we think we are already awake, it doesn't make much sense to be told to awaken. The Work is about raising our consciousness, and talks about different states of consciousness. The first is when we are actually asleep. The second is when we wake from our sleep. We think we are awake but are still in a state of sleep, hypnotized by almost everything. The Work refers to this state as the "so-called waking state." We eat, play, work, and even write books, such as this one, but we are in the state of waking-sleep.

We do everything mechanically in the only way we can do it. Our various 'I's run our lives and we think they are our real selves. Not only do we think that we are awake when we are in the "so-called waking state," but we do not realize that this "so-called waking state" is a prison from which we must escape in order to experience real freedom. If, however, we think we are free, then it seems awfully stupid to think we have to try to escape. Moreover, the only way we can escape from this prison is either to be guided by someone who has escaped, or to follow the Work or other true teachings. First we have to realize we are in a prison before we can even think about escaping.

The best description of our actual situation is the cave allegory in Plato's *Republic*. In this allegory, men are chained in a cave and all they see are the shadows reflected on the wall behind them. They believe these shadows are what reality is. When one of them escapes and gets above ground and sees that shadows are not the actual reality and then goes back into the cave and reports his findings to the other chained prisoners, none of them believe him.

This is why the Good Householders with a Magnetic Center are the only ones who can really change. They realize that any change they make in their external circumstances is not going to solve their problems. By having a Magnetic Center they become open to B influences—influences outside of life. By coming under these B influences or teachings, they develop a screen to shield them from the ups and downs of life that are inevitable under A influences, which come from life.

Of course, I can hear the reader thinking to himself while reading the above discussion that the notion of man awakening from his sleep and actually still being asleep is a ridiculous idea. (I thought the same thing when I first heard this Work idea). What does the Work mean when it says the person is still asleep? I can ask him a question, and he answers me. He sees the red light, and he doesn't cross the street, or stops his vehicle if driving. How can he be asleep? This whole idea is absurd; it's pure nonsense. The Work would agree that it is non-sense. On the sensory level he is not asleep. If we leave the sensory level and look at him at a deeper psychological and spiritual level he is asleep because he never remembers himself, and neither do we.

What Is Self-Remembering?

One of the key elements of the Work is that we do not remember ourselves, and the Work is about bringing us into that state—that is, the third state of consciousness where we do remember ourselves. Let us suppose an actor, George Brown, is playing a role on the stage. He is very involved in playing the role of Joe Smith, villain, or playing Jesus in the Passion Play. Sometimes the actor must remember himself and think, I am not Joe Smith, the villain, or Jesus. I am George Brown. He must separate himself from the role he is playing because, obviously, the role is a temporary identity he has taken on. It is not his true self.

Perhaps this is why actors like to play different roles so they

41

don't get typecast in any particular role. Of more importance, the actor doesn't want to adopt in real life the persona he or she is playing on the stage or in the movie. Perhaps the actor always is playing tough guys on the screen and starts to adopt this tough guy attitude in real life. In a movie, which is made in bits and pieces, this problem may not be as serious as when an actor gives a complete performance in a play over and over again. A good example of someone not remembering himself can be seen in the movie *Jesus of Montreal*, where a young actor plays Jesus in the passion play. He doesn't remember himself and starts acting as if he were Jesus. He goes to an audition for some advertisers and starts overturning tables as Jesus did in the temple.

The trick is to remember that the part we are playing in life is not our real self; it is just a part, as with the actor on the stage. We do have a real self, called Real 'I', but it can never develop if we keep thinking that what we are doing is our real self. Since we lack unity and have various 'I's or personalities that are doing different things (often contradictory to each other), we get caught in the belief, when acting, that each 'I' is our real self. What we should be saying, as the Work points out, is "There goes Friedman again. This is not the real me." Whatever our name is, as we go through the day, we should try saying to ourselves, "There goes Johnson; this is not the real me." Otherwise, we will never remember ourselves and, as with the actor in *Jesus of Montreal*, we will believe we are the part we are playing.

What Keeps Us from Self-Remembering?
1. Identification

Probably the biggest obstacle to remembering ourselves is identification. As with the actor in *Jesus of Montreal*, who started to believe and act as if he were Jesus outside of the play, we identify with the events in our lives and become one with them, and our real self disappears. The person whose whole identity is tied up with his finances might commit suicide when, for example, he loses all of his money. This was not uncommon during the great Depression in the 1930s. We become whatever we have identified with. If we have an illness and all we do is think about it, we become the illness. We might be thinking, "Well if I have a financial problem or an illness, it is only natural that I think about it." The important point to realize is that becoming identified with a problem or situation is not something we do consciously after pondering the situation. We do it automatically, instantaneously. We are not merely thinking about the subject, we become obsessed with it. It usually impairs our ability to think and act logically about the particular matter we are identified with.

An analogy that Nicoll used is a pool table. On the table are six pockets that the balls can drop into, one at each of the corners and two on the sides. When we become identified with the events of life, it is as if we fell into one of the pockets. The rest of the world disappears. We can no longer see the sun, trees, and skies. We leave the here and now and worry about the past or the future. We are totally absorbed by what we have become identified with, and what we have identified with has power over us. The whole purpose of the Work or any system of psycho-transformation is to realize we are self-developing beings, working consciously against the circumstances of our lives and thereby avoid going into negative states. The Work provides a shield that separates life's events and us. Otherwise, we continually get knocked into the pockets. Through the Work, we can raise our consciousness and awareness and be in the here and now more often.

One of the main features about being identified is that we always feel it is justified under the circumstances. In this particular circumstance, we think we have a right to be identified. The only problem with this is that we usually go from one to another. If, for example, we cure the particular illness we presently have, we then become identified with the next problem, maybe another health issue, or some other problem and forget all about what we were once identified with.

As Mark Twain once commented, "Ninety percent of the things he worried about never happened." Ninety percent of the things we identify with are solved or go away by themselves. The point is that when we are identified, we do not realize we are identified, and we disappear into whatever it is we have identified with. We are not even aware that we are identified with a problem—we just become that problem.

In my opinion, to be in a state of nonidentification is to be in bliss. We know there are problems in our life, but we keep them from dominating us and can maintain a state of calm joy because we are not being "eaten up" by our problems. A sentence in the Buddhist Metta, a scriptural narrative on kindness says, "Let one not be submerged by the things of the world." The fact is that most of the time we are continually submerged or identified with the external events of life. Sometimes I tell myself to take a half-hour vacation from my problems. It sometimes works and indeed feels very good. Even being aware that we are identified is a big step forward in the work on ourselves, even if we can't stop the identification. This will be discussed later on. We will also discuss what some of the consequences are of all the devices we use that keep us from remembering ourselves.

2. Internal Considering vs. External Considering

A second method that keeps us from remembering ourselves is to be constantly internally considering. The Work distinguishes between internal considering and external considering. In external considering we put ourselves in the shoes of another person. We try to see why he or she is acting as they are. We try to see the other's point of view. This leads to harmonious relationships. Furthermore, to go deeper into external considering we try to find in ourselves what we dislike in the other person. To do this we have to expand our consciousness to look for these traits in ourselves. The third result of external considering is that if we do this we begin to see we are not the person we imagine ourselves to be. We thought, for example, we were always honest, but we see in certain situations that we are not as honest as we imagined ourselves to be. We therefore obtain a truer picture of ourselves.

Internal considering, on the other hand, is when we always see things from our point of view. Internal considering has two sides to the same coin. The first is that we are not treated as we think we should be. We have been wronged in some way. We feel people do not respect us enough; they hurt our feelings. We take everything personally. Anytime we feel offended, we can take that as a signal that we will start internal considering. If we cannot stop this internal considering, the more it will grow and spread over all areas of our life. Furthermore, the more requirements we make of life and wanting things in certain ways, the more disappointments we will have and, therefore, the more internal considering we will engage in. Internal considering is not something we decide to do; it is a mechanical, automatic reaction when things don't go the way we wish they would.

When we internally consider, we go around having conversations with ourselves over the wrongs that have been committed against us, or the acts that should have been done for us, or that were unjustly done to us; it was unfair. Life, in general, has been unfair to us. We deserve better. We expect too much. Someone or something is always "doing us wrong," even natural events, such as the weather spoiling our picnic or vacation.

The other side of the coin of internal considering is that we start to make plans to get even with the party who has wronged us. The sequence is that, first, a man becomes identified with himself, and then he becomes offended and upset because he has been "wronged." Then he starts "making accounts." These inner accounts consist of imaginary conversations going on continuously in our minds. We have all sorts of things we want to say to others and think of how we are going to give them "a piece of our mind" when we see them again.

In the Work, there is a concept called "Singing your Song." This refers not to a physical song, but a psychological song. Everyone has his or her song. It is what they repeat over and over again in their heads and sing out loud when with others. For some, it is that life isn't fair. For others it is that no one understands the difficulties they face. Other songs could be about how badly they have been treated, how they married the wrong person, or how they have not been appreciated. There are literally thousands of these psychological songs that are sung over and over again.

The Work also talks about "good singers," those people who sing their psychological song at the drop of a hat and never can get beyond themselves. For some, one or two drinks will allow them to go into their song. For some, just greeting them will bring on their song. Moreover, people sing their song not only to others but when they are by themselves. What is your song? While writing this, I realized that one of my songs is that Friedman always has a physical complaint he is singing about. These songs are the negative messages we sing to ourselves over and over again. And, of course, some people have several songs, or a whole repertory of songs they sing to themselves just as professional singers have a repertory of songs they sing. I wonder how many other songs I have that I don't realize are in my repertory. "Singing your Song" always involves somehow blaming others or the world at large for our condition. According to the Work, one cannot grow if one is singing his song and blaming.

The songs that we sing to ourselves and are not aware we are singing are difficult to discover. The Work refers to these as our inner secret songs. These are the songs that we do not sing to others, but that we often sing to ourselves when we are alone and are not aware we are singing them. For example, we can be in bad moods, making it unpleasant to be by ourselves. These inner secret songs poison our psychological space. They cause us untold suffering. Only by deep self-observation can we observe and therefore discover our "inner secret songs."

There is only one antidote to "singing your songs" and our inner secret songs and that is gratitude. Gratitude is the secret balm that can cure all our songs and is the antidote to our making accounts. When we consider what a miracle it is that we even reached adulthood, with all the near misses the vast majority of us had growing up, we can give thanks for what we have, and get over what we think we need to become complete. Without gratitude we will always be making account of what we are owed.

The Work states that we can grow only when we forgive all others because they are doing the best they can under the circumstances. This is external considering. External considering as opposed to internal considering does not happen automatically, mechanically. We have to make a conscious effort to see the matter from another's point of view. According to the Work, however, we are all machines, not conscious beings. We do all things mechanically.

Therefore, we should not be surprised or upset when people do not behave as we desire.

There is an old Zen story on this point. A man is in a rowboat on a foggy lake. He notices through the fog that a boat is coming towards him. He tries to row away from the boat and yells in the direction of the boat for its occupant to change direction. The boat continues on its straight course toward the boat. Finally, the boats collide; the other boat was empty of any occupants. It was just drifting. It was moving mechanically through the water. We, according to the Work, are moving mechanically through life. People, at least most people, won't yell at a radio that doesn't work, so why yell at people who are just as mechanical as the radio? Our problem is that we think people, including ourselves, are conscious. This idea that we are machines and therefore not conscious of what we do or why we do it, was said in a different way by Mark Twain, who commented, "When one remembers we are all mad, the mystery disappears and life stands explained."

3. Self-Justification

Another variation of internal considering is self-justification. If something has not gone as we thought it should, we spend our time in endless self-justification for what we did or omitted to do, so we don't have to take responsibility for it. We tend to blame others or the situation and end up in the state of internal considering.

4. Self-Pity

This is just the opposite of self-justification. Instead of trying to justify what we did or did not do, we feel sorry for ourselves. Poor me! No one understands me; and we wallow in our own self-pity. It is somehow a delicious, if perverse, feeling and we often don't want to give it up. Both self-justification and self-pity are forms of identification because in these states we do not remember ourselves.

What Are Some of the Consequences
of Not-Remembering Ourselves?
The First Consequence is it Leads to Being in a Negative State

Gurdjieff said that what makes the world go round is negative emotions. The world is awash with them. Gurdjieff also said that the easiest thing is to be negative. Negativity is very contagious. We heard it all around us as we grew up. Our parents and others in our environment were finding fault, if not with us then with each other, neighbors, or the world.

When we are identified with a problem or a situation, we turn negative. We worry about it. We are overcome by our difficulties. When we are negative, we have a poison in our psychological bodies that poisons all our thoughts and our relationships. Being negative also creates tension in our bodies and causes illness. The continuously hostile person is more likely to have heart attacks and other health problems than one who isn't hostile. What could be more negative than being continually hostile and angry all the time?

The Second Consequence is We Lose Force

We know how after worrying about something constantly or after having an argument, we often feel exhausted. The reason is that we have lost force. Force is the amount of energy we have at our disposal. Let's suppose we gave a numerical value to force and say every day one wakes up with 100 units. This would be the energy to get through the day. If, before we even get out of bed in the morning, we are worrying or dreading some event, we can lose much of our 100 units of force before we even get out of bed. If, when we get out of bed, we have an argument with someone over breakfast, we can lose more of our force. So before we leave home, we could have lost our force for the day.

On the other hand, let us say we have neutral thoughts when we awake. Then we would lose no force upon arising. If we have positive thoughts about what the day will bring and feel good, we might even accumulate some force before we get out of bed and have more than 100 units of force for the day. If, at the breakfast table and wherever we are during the day, we hold off saying something negative or do something to avoid a confrontation, we will have gained force. No, we cannot avoid an argument or a confrontation mechanically. Mechanically, it is just too easy to be negative, to give that person who deserves it "a piece of our mind." We might feel good in that instant, but we start to feel lousy fairly quickly. We have lost force.

We want to preserve our force. If we can do things that avoid the confrontation or argument and don't give the person, who we honestly think deserves it, "a piece of our mind," through conscious restraint we will gain force and have better relationships. As Harlan Miller once observed about marriage, "Often the difference between a successful marriage and a mediocre one consists of leaving about three or four things a day unsaid."

Force is very important because the Work says that to do any conscious work on our development, we have to accumulate it. If we constantly lose force up by becoming angry, being in arguments, taking everything personally and always being identified, we will have no force to work on our own development. Moreover, by always wasting our force we will be exhausted, find it difficult to do the things we have to do to get through the day, and have no force left for the things we want to do.

Even the simple little things can exhaust our force. We are about to leave home, and we look for our keys or wallet and we can't find them. We are already running a little late. We are frustrated. We become angry and may use the language that we feel is appropriate to express our frustration. We finally find the keys or wallet, but it is obvious we have lost force in the process. Thus, the Work emphasizes the conservation and building up of force for work on our transformation, rather than leaking it all the time. We can leak force from ourselves just as water can leak into a boat. If we have to spend much of our time bailing the water from a leaky boat, it will make it harder to reach our destination, just as continually leaking our force will make it difficult for us to develop ourselves.

Another way we can lose force is when we attach too much importance to something of no great importance. We loose our ability to laugh, especially at ourselves, and everything becomes serious: for example, the delay in having our meal served in a restaurant, or which brand of toothpaste to buy, or continually arranging the papers on our desk before we actually get down to the necessary project we have to work on. This depletes force. So knowing what is important and not important is crucial. In fact, the Work states that lack of seeing the relative importance of things is a sign of stupidity, and intelligence is being able to see things in their relative order of importance. That is why we must prioritize and reprioritize continually to get done what is really important to us and not waste our time and force on the unessential.

Prioritizing and re-prioritizing also brings up the concept of scale in the Work. Things are on different levels or scales, and the scale we are on has a large effect on how we handle things. For example, we may have personal worries and problems that we constantly identify with. When, however, a national emergency develops such as an earthquake, tornado, or the 9/11 terrorist attack, our personal problems do not concern us nearly as much. This is because we are involved with something on a much higher scale than our personal problems, and we act in a much nobler fashion than we ordinarily do. In terms of the Work in these situations, we are much more likely to externally consider than internally consider. And when we externally consider rather than internally consider, we are much less likely to become negative and resort to violence.

The Third Consequence is We Become Violent

The Work states that negative emotions always lead to violence. The violence may not be physical, but of a verbal nature. In the animal kingdom during the mating season, jealousy—a negative emotion—leads to violence. Often the weaker male is punished severely, occasionally even by death in the fight to mate with the female. With man, physical violence may not be as prevalent in our individual lives, but verbal violence is quite common.

Let us consider how internal considering can lead to verbal violence. Suppose, for example, we have an appointment with someone who is late. We start a dialogue in our mind about how this person doesn't respect us: he is always late, and it isn't fair that this person is abusing us by keeping us waiting. He knows how we hate to wait. This is the last time we will ever make an appointment with him, and so on. We never consider the fact that this person has been late before, customarily comes late for all his appointments, and most likely will be late today. Moreover, we have brought nothing to read while waiting for this person. Therefore, because of this inner dialogue of internal considering when he does show up, instead of enjoying the time together, the person who was kept waiting blows up (i.e., becomes violent verbally) and ruins the time together. Or, if we do not start an argument, we resent the person and thus still spoil our time with him.

A classic situation of this is when, as adults, we make a phone call to one of our parents. Instead of enjoying the conversation, the parent often says, "Why have you waited so long to call?" It has been two days, or two weeks, or two months, or two years, and the parent has been internally considering why we're not calling regularly. Therefore, when we do call, the first thing said is the fact that we haven't called earlier. If this internal considering had not been going on before we called, it wouldn't be the first thing that jumps out of their mouths. When this happens, we end up spending a good part of the telephone call trying to defend ourselves, and it leaves a bad taste for both people, often breeding ill will rather than affection. We think, "That's the last time I'll call him (or her) for a while."

This also illustrates another point in the Work: everything that manifests itself in life is caused by the un-manifested, by a thought in our mind. For example, before the house—the manifest—is built, someone must have an idea of the house—the un-manifested—in their mind. Before we become verbally abusive (the manifest), we have done some internal considering in our minds (the un-manifested). If we didn't internally consider the situation, we would not have become verbally abusive.

There is one other point that the Work makes that is different from society's general view. We might have bad thoughts about someone or consider actions we would like to take against someone that are not positive. However, as long as we don't say what we feel to the other person or act the way we would like to, it is considered okay by most people or at least better than actually saying or doing these acts. In the Work, bad thoughts we would like to say or harmful action are just as bad as actually saying the words or committing the acts. We must cleanse ourselves of these thoughts because they poison us. They are all part of internal considering, the making of accounts against the other person, and, whether we actually say them or just think them, they are doing us harm and are a loss of force and lead to violence.

The Fourth Consequence is
We Lose Contact with Our Higher Centers

Perhaps, the most serious consequence of not remembering ourselves is that by being in a negative state we shut ourselves off from contact with Higher Centers within us that try to guide us. These Higher Centers are reflected in our intuition, hunches that we get as to what to do, or seeing solutions we had not thought of before. The static from the negative states is like the static on the radio that prevents us from hearing a program clearly. If we want, we can substitute "intuition" or "God" for Higher Centers that the Work uses; they are the same. Being negative prevents us from receiving guidance from a higher source. The main point is that because of this static, we cannot develop ourselves.

The Work says we have two births. The first is when we are born into a physical body; the second is when we awaken and start the long process of developing ourselves and raising our level of being. Since our level of being attracts what happens to us, only by personal transformation can we change our level of being and subsequently change the circumstances of our life. So if we are always in a negative state, we block any chance of transformation. We are stuck where we are. If we were happy with ourselves, we would not need to develop ourselves. Thus, it is only people who are unhappy in their present life situation who become interested in any of the various forms of self-transformation, whether they be the Work or any of the other forms of meditation and self-transformation. If we are always in a negative state, no matter how much knowledge we take in, we are not able to apply it in our lives because the guidance to act and apply that knowledge for change is blocked by our negative state. We have too much static in our psychological space.

How the Work Views Man: Personality and Essence

The Work says that man has two parts: essence and personality. We are born with essence. It is what we receive from the heavens. Essence is our true nature. Only by uncovering our essence can we change our being. Essence only obeys the truth. It can never succeed through lies. When we are very young, up to three or four years old, our true essence is present. However, we also have personality.

At first, personality is very weak, but in time it becomes very powerful and completely submerges our essence. Personality grows through what we are told as we grow up and what we observe and follow. If we hear negativity all around us as we grow up, it is only natural that our personality becomes negative. Our views on life, opinions, and judgments about things are all from personality. The Work says we need to develop personality so that we can make it in the world. Personality gives us the strength to earn our way and get along in the world. However, once we have made it in the world, for our second birth to begin, our long-neglected essence must start to grow at the expense of personality. This is very difficult. Personality dominates us, yet our essence can still emerge.

We all probably have heard accounts of persons whose families were all lawyers or physicians and they pressured their son or daughter to follow the family footsteps. After a few or many years in the profession, the person, let's say the son, feels this just isn't right for him. He gives up his career and lucrative income to open a garden shop because he loves plants or does something else that he feels much more comfortable in. This is the essence coming through. Perhaps his whole personality changes. He is no longer the life of the party and becomes much quieter. People who know him might say he is not as interesting as he was before, but the people who make these changes toward their true selves, their essences, feel much more at peace with themselves than when their personality dominated them.

It is a long struggle to allow our true essence to once again arise and become dominant and let personality slide into the background and become more passive. Personality does not want to give up its superior position to essence very easily. It fights very hard to maintain its dominance over essence. The Work states it has two tools that help it maintain its dominance over essence: False Personality and Imaginary 'I'.

What Does the Work Say About False Personality
and Imaginary 'I'?

Imaginary 'I' is the idea that we have a single unified 'I' or really permanent personality. This 'I' always answers consciously, and behaves consciously and consistently. It is an illusion that prevents us from seeing the contradictions of the various 'I's we have. We can do this because the buffers that we discussed earlier do not let us see our various contradictions.

The Imaginary 'I' leads us to develop False Personality, which gives us wrong ideas and a wrong opinion of ourselves. It claims it has all sorts of abilities and talents we really do not have. It gives us false pictures of ourselves, imaginary ideas of ourselves, and imaginary fantasies of ourselves. Suppose, for example, a man is a civil engineer. This is a skill he has learned in order to get along in the world, and it is part of his personality. If this civil engineer thinks he is the best civil engineer in the world, this is part of his false personality. False Personality is the unreal thing in us.

Another way to think of False Personality is to think of it as the face we present to the World to reflect ourselves. For example, for some it is "poor little me," and we want the world to feel sorry for us. For others, the picture could be what a generous person I am, and we want the world to acknowledge how generous and noble we are.

For others it could be a "self-depreciating humor" that makes fun of ourselves as a way to ingratiate ourselves with others. It is the Woody Allen-type role, and I find that I have adopted this False

Personality for myself. It took me a long time to get a glimpse of it, and I started taking mental photographs of it in various situations. It became quite obvious to me, although it was probably obvious to others for a long time. I still haven't been able to change, but at least I am aware of this aspect of my False Personality and have increased my consciousness about how I behave. The fact is that none of these pictures we present to the world are true; they are the shield behind which we hide and prevent our Real 'I' from coming out and further keep our essence submerged.

One of the goals of the Work is to get to our real selves, our Real 'I'. All these pretenses we carry prevent us from getting to our Real 'I'. It is hard to see our own pretenses, but easier to see the False Personality in others when they speak with false intonations and use false gestures and expressions. One way the Work says we know we are in False Personality is that we always want praise for what we do. When we see we are looking for praise from others we know we are in False Personality.

When we are in False Personality, we are always involved with our exterior reality, with the senses. We cannot enter our interior (our psychological side), so our being escapes us. We are totally involved with outward appearances. False Personality gives us an entirely unreal existence and attracts only unreal things. In short, False Personality makes us identify with what is not ourselves and so makes us unhappy.

The Work states that the two companions of False Personality are Vanity and Pride. Vanity always wants to be first, such as the mother of the disciples James and John who requested that they sit on the right and left of Jesus in the Kingdom. Pride will lie to be first, such as the disciple Peter who said he would never betray Jesus and then did. With all these difficulties that we have around us, the question is how can we change?

How Can We Change?

Although the summary of some of the concepts in the Work expressed so far are much less involved and simplified than the complexity of the Work itself, it is time to ask the main question of the Work and all other esoteric systems: How can one change? What makes the Work different from other methods of transformation and makes change possible are the tools it uses. I believe it is the emphasis on our negative states. Unless we realize how much of our life is spent being negative we cannot get out of these negative states. The foremost tool for noticing our negative states and our chance of transforming them to positive states is self-observation or noticing of oneself. No one can do this for us, not a leader, teacher, or minister. Only we can do it for ourselves. Only by our own effort can we lift ourselves up to a higher state of being. Therefore, many people do not like the Work and drop out shortly after they start because they realize that no one is going to do the Work for them.

A teacher can definitely help because he or she has found the way out. The allegory the Work uses is that we are all in prison but don't realize it, and only someone who has realized he is in prison and finds a way out can help us. Although such a person can definitely help, in the final analysis only we ourselves can do the digging, making the effort to get out of the prison we are in. The primary tool of the Work is observation. First we must distinguish between internal and external observation.

External and Internal Observation or Attention

The Work says there are two kinds of paying attention or observing things. We can use our eyes, ears and other senses to observe our environment. This is external attention. Naturalists are specialists observing or attending to plants and animals with their senses and making careful observations about what they see.

Internal attention is when we observe or attend to what is going on inside of us. Do we ever ask ourselves what our state is at this particular moment? Are we happy, depressed, or sad? Although it might be hard to know what psychological state we are in, we can infer it by the way we are acting if we observe ourselves. If we are slumped, our head down and shoulders rounded, we are in a depressed state. If we are moving strongly, making decisive motions and humming a tune, we are obviously in a happy state. By changing our body motions it is possible to change the psychological state we are in. If we are feeling low, a brisk walk will make us feel better, and therefore change our psychological state.

When we identify with problems that consume us, we block everything else out both externally and internally and feel we are nothing but what we have identified with, such as an illness. We are often so involved in internal considering by having an imaginary conversation with someone and giving this other person "a piece of our mind" that we don't see anything on the outside except the bare minimum to avoid an accident. And sometimes we can't even avoid the accident because we are so involved with internal considering. We all can attend to the external world, but many of us are so identified with what is currently happening inside us that we rarely see what is outside us. We walk down streets or country roads and do not see much at all because we are so identified by what is going on within us.

The Work is about changing our state by means of self-observation, not by changing our external circumstances. We have tried changing our external circumstances but these changes have not affected our psychological state. The Work says that what we are in life—happy or unhappy—is dependent on our psychological state, not on our external circumstances. The key is not what happens to us, but how we react to what happens to us. The way we react is our life. A man can be a multi-millionaire who worries all the time about his assets going up or down and who reacts harshly to those who work for him, and to his family. Such a man is unhappy despite his vast wealth. He is poor in spirit. What this man needs is a change in his attitude toward life, not accumulating more wealth.

What Is Involved In Self-Observation?

If we are going to change we must know what we are going to change from. We have to know how we presently are, how we act, think, and feel. The only way we can do this is through self-observation.

Ouspensky discussed four factors that keep us from observing ourselves. One is constant talking in which we talk mechanically, not thinking about what we are saying. If we talk ceaselessly, we prevent ourselves from ever looking inward to observe ourselves. The second is lying. If we constantly tell lies to others as well as to ourselves we can never see what is actually happening to us because these lies prevent us from seeing what is really there. The third factor is imagination, the mechanical imagination where our minds flitter in an undirected manner and we fantasize about all sorts of things. These fantasies keep us from being able to see what we are actually like. Negative imagination is particularly harmful because we keep imagining the worst possible scenario, and this prevents us from making a true assessment of the situation. The fourth factor is negative emotions. When we are experiencing negative emotions, we distort everything. It is like looking at one of those funny mirrors where we are either elongated or made rounder than we are. The negative emotions distort everything so that we are prevented from actually observing accurately how we are.

According to the Work, the main requirement for self-observation is to separate into two people: the observed and the observer. If we cannot make this separation, we will find it impossible to observe ourselves because we think there is nothing to observe. So I must separate myself from Friedman, and you must separate yourself from Johnson or Jones or whatever your name is. Therefore, I watch Friedman go through his little acts and foibles. My goal is at first not to change Friedman, but just to observe how he behaves. Friedman is the personality I have accumulated, consisting of layers of overcoats, an analogy that Ouspensky used, that I have put on myself that hide my Real 'I'. So I want to get to know how Friedman behaves in various situations. If I make no separation between Friedman and the real me, it is impossible to observe him. Only by realizing Friedman is not the real me can I even start to make attempts to observe Friedman.

Self-observation has two effects. One is to shed light on how we are, to place the light of consciousness on ourselves. Suppose we wanted to enter a dark room with which we were not familiar. We would turn the light on before we entered, and if we didn't even know where the light switch was, we could use a flashlight to find our way around the room. By throwing the light of consciousness on ourselves and seeing how we really are, we can obtain a picture of ourselves. The second function of self-observation is that sometimes the light of consciousness will in itself change things. There is a Stop exercise in the Work where Gurdjieff would say, "Stop," and his students would have to hold their position exactly, including facial expression, and even their thoughts, until Gurdjieff released them. By doing this numerous times, his students came to see how they really behaved and thought. Over a certain period of time these Stops formed a composite photograph of how people really were.

One thing that the Work realizes is that we cannot observe ourselves all the time. Rather, we have moments during the day when we do consciously observe ourselves. These isolated moments become a Work memory. If we have enough of them, we can form a composite picture, a mental photograph of how we do think and act. By conscious observations of ourselves, we can eventually have a whole photo album of mental photographs of how we think and act in various situations.

It is these composite photographs that give us a chance to become aware of how we actually think and act and are therefore the basis of making changes in ourselves. Unless we can develop these composite photographs, we can never get a true picture of how we are. If, for example, we consider ourselves honest, the next time the clerk in the checkout line makes an error in our favor and we are aware of it, and we let it go, we just keep that little snapshot in our mind, to help form the picture of how we really are. Before discussing further anything we can observe, we should consider some of the Work's "no-no's" of self-observation.

The "No-No's" of Self-Observation

Self-observation must be done objectively, or it loses all value. If we criticize ourselves while observing ourselves, we go into another negative state. Thus, if we happen to be at the checkout line and the clerk makes an error in our favor and we do nothing to correct it, criticizing ourselves will only make matters worse because we have identified again with the situation. It is much better to say, "There goes Friedman again," or "There goes Johnson again." And our picture of ourselves as an always-honest man or woman will come into its true light. We will get a small snapshot of how we really are in regard to our picture of ourselves as an honest person.

Another thing that will destroy the quality of our self-

66

observation is by justifying our actions. Self-justification is another way to keep from observing ourselves and seeing how we really are. For example, after we leave the store, or even when we let the error in our favor go by, we start self-justifying the action by rationalizing that the store is a very big chain and very wealthy. They'll never miss the little change we got away with. Besides, they charge outrageous prices and the checkout line was so long because there weren't enough check stands open.

We can also feel sorry for ourselves and be in a state of self-pity. Poor me, I have so little and the owners of this giant chain have so much. All methods of identification, such as self-justification or self-pity, destroy the quality of our self-observing because they put us in a negative state.

Another no-no of self-observation is to analyze why we do what we do, or why we act as we act. The Work asks us to just observe our actions without trying to analyze them. From the Work point of view, the cause of the negative emotion is not examined, but the fact that we are negative is what is important. The Work hopes that, some day, after much observation, we can separate from those particular actions and negative states.

The Work asks us not to take ourselves so seriously. Observation of ourselves especially will help if we are not so serious, and can even have a sense of humor about it. For example, "There goes Friedman again with his cold in which he is miserable and will never recover from;" or "There goes Friedman unable to make a decision again."

So let us go back to our mundane example at the checkout counter. We let an error in our favor to go by. We don't criticize ourselves but we are observing that we are not quite as honest as we pictured ourselves to be. We don't analyze to see what in our past development caused us to allow an error in our favor go by. Then this same sort of incident happens again. We also let the error in our favor slide by. After these events happen several or maybe many times, we notice without criticizing ourselves that something, an internal taste, is taking place.

The Taste of the Work

After this happens several times, we notice we have a bad taste in our mouth. This taste does not feel right and it stays with us. We are not critical; we are just observing it. It stays with us for a while. Then when we are in the same situation again when the error goes in our favor, we notify the clerk, and it is corrected. After the correction, we do not get the bad taste in our mouth. We might, in fact, have a good taste. The important thing is that we know by the taste of our actions what is true and false. The Work says that this may take years. There are no easy shortcuts and we just have to observe ourselves without criticism, self-justification, internal considering, self-pity, or analysis, and with a sense of humor as to what we have observed to obtain a picture of what type of person we really are. Only when we have this picture of ourselves can we start to change. We must not only observe our inner states, but we must also observe our different centers.

Observing Our Centers

According to the Work, not only do we have many personalities and lack unity, but we also have different centers. Each of us has four centers: Intellectual, Emotional, Moving, and Instinctive/Sex. Each of these centers exerts a tremendous influence over us because when we act, what we do depends on which center is acting.

Each center has a definite function. The Intellectual Center makes comparisons. One object is bigger or smaller than another. Whenever we are making a comparison or judgment of any sort, we are using our Intellectual Center. The Emotional Center either likes or dislikes something. So whenever we like something or dislike something, we are using our Emotional Center. The Moving Center contains all we have learned. Things such as learning to drive a car and using a computer and even the multiplication tables are in the Moving Center. The Instinctive/Sex Center contains what was given to us. We all have the ability to breathe, to digest our food, and to have our blood circulate. These activities all fall within the Instinctive/Sex Center. Sometimes the Instinctive/Sex Center is combined with the Moving Center for some purposes because they are much closer to each other than they are to the Intellectual and Emotional Centers.

Each center is divided into divisions so that the Intellectual Center has not only an Intellectual Division but an Emotional Division and a Moving Division as well. Different divisions of these centers carry on different functions of the Intellectual Center. This, of course, like all aspects of the Work, is very dense and has many layers of meaning.

There is a concept in the Work referred to as "the wrong work of centers." Each center is best suited for certain tasks. Often, however, Centers take over tasks that they are not well suited for, which results in our functioning at below optimum levels, e.g., walking down a flight of stairs and starting to think about which foot we are going to place down next. This is using our Intellectual Center when the Moving Center knows exactly what needs to be done. It is the wrong work of the Intellectual Center. The same would apply to riding a bicycle. Once we learn how to balance ourselves on the bike, this information is lodged in our Moving Center. To think about how we should balance ourselves on the bike with our Intellectual Center is again the wrong work of this Center.

It also explains why once we have learned to ride a bike, even after many years of not riding one, we can get on the bike and ride. The information to ride is stored in the Moving Center. One doesn't have to think about how to do it. Good dancers do not look at their feet while dancing. They know intuitively that their feet know what to do. They use their Moving Centers. Bad dancers look at their feet constantly, thinking they can control their feet by thinking about what their feet are doing. These are all examples of wrong work of the Intellectual Center. On the other hand, if someone must make a decision about something he feels is important in his life, and he feels rushed and feels that he must make this decision immediately, then this would be the wrong work of the Moving Center.

These centers must also cooperate with each other as with, for example, a smoker who wants to stop. This is a decision made with his Intellectual Center. A few hours or minutes after making his decision, he reaches almost unconsciously for a cigarette and starts smoking. The problem is that his Emotional Center, which still likes smoking, was not considered in his original decision to quit. Therefore, even though his Intellectual Center thought it was the right thing to do logically, his Emotional Center won't go along with it, and he continues to smoke. As a professor of mine used to comment, "Logic is good for the mind but not for the guts."

If we want to make a change we have to have more than just our Intellectual Center involved. It is crucial that our Emotional Center, which is much stronger and much faster acting than our Intellectual Center, get involved in any change we think about making. That is why we may have picked up a cigarette just a few moments after our Intellectual Center said we wanted to quit. This is why most New Year's resolutions dissipate so quickly. Only the Intellectual Center was involved in making them. We must get our Emotional Center revved up and feeling very strongly about something before we can change it. Otherwise, no change will take place—or if it does, it will not last. We have to awaken our Buried Conscience.

The Concept of Buried Conscience

The Work says we have two types of conscience. One is acquired conscience that comes from our training and social customs and is different in different countries and in different regions of the

71

same country. In some places, violence is always bad, while in other places not taking vengeance if a family member is harmed goes against the acquired conscience.

The Work says that, as opposed to this, we have a real or Buried Conscience that is the same for everyone. It is buried deep in our Emotional Center and is out of reach. Buried Conscience is what allows us to change our Emotional Center. With Buried Conscience we know what is good and true. It gives us an inner taste by which we can judge our emotions. It knows that being in negative states is neither true nor good. Buried Conscience connects us with our Higher Emotional Center that has been cut off by all the negativity we have acquired by habit, dominating our Emotional Center.

The ideas of the Work are brought into our Intellectual Center. If we like them, they settle in the emotions branch of the Intellectual Center. This then stimulates the Buried Conscience in the Emotional Center, and we begin to develop an inner taste to help us determine which of our actions and emotions are good and which are bad. Those that give us a good inner taste are the ones that bring us happiness. Without this Buried Conscience that can fight the general negativity we have acquired in our Emotional Center, there could be no change from being negative. With it, we can start to change. Our guideline will be the inner taste of our actions.

What Changes are Important from the Work Point of View?

When people talk about making changes, they are usually on the physical level. People want to lose weight, stop smoking, or start exercising. Others want to earn more money; some yearn to be free of their present jobs. These are all very visible goals. The Work says that changing these habits or goals, which admittedly is very difficult, will not accomplish any change in a person's level of being.

In fact, as Gurdjieff points out, curing one habit might lead to a worse one because nothing has changed in the person. It is compared in the Work to pushing a physical bulge in one place and it comes out in another. The person does stop smoking and shortly afterwards gains a large amount of weight. The person stops drinking and becomes much more quarrelsome and more trouble to the people he lives with than when he was drinking. Moreover, even if one successfully eliminates his habit without replacing it with another one, he is still dissatisfied with himself because on a psychological level he is still the same.

The Work states that it is more important to make changes on the psychological level than on the physical one. The psychological level is where we live, and therefore, can affect changes in our being. If our being changes, it will attract different things into our life. So what are some of the psychological changes the Work talks about? They all start with self-observation, so we can actually see the type of person we are and eventually see some of our buffers that keep us from seeing various sides of ourselves.

We can practice complaining less about the conditions in our lives. We can observe how we continually internally consider and make accounts and try to stop. We can observe we identify that we worry about anything that has happened or that we think will happen to us. We can notice how we self-justify everything and try to stop it.

Let us start with complaining. First, we realize that without complaining, there would be little for most people to talk about. Susan Jeffers, in her book *Feel the Fear and Do It Anyway*, gave one of her classes an assignment for one week of not complaining about anything. The students came back claiming that they had nothing to say during the week. So much of our conversations concern complaining.

If we want to try an experiment and apply the Work, the next time we are in a conversation and someone is criticizing something, or someone, we can see if we are able to withhold our criticism. It is much more difficult than we might think. We have to remember ourselves to do this. The problem with being negative, such as continually complaining, is that we lose force or energy. To do this Work, we have to accumulate energy to make greater efforts than the efforts needed to get by in life. If we withhold the criticism or complaint, we will gain force or energy. We will also feel better. Whether we can control our complaining and other negative states depends upon our knowing the difference between knowing and understanding.

The Difference Between Knowing and Understanding

The Work says that we can know a lot and understand very little, and on the other hand we can know very little and understand much. Just knowing the concepts discussed in the Work, having a notebook full of the ideas, reading Gurdjieff, Ouspensky, and their students' books on the Work, does not mean we understand the concepts of the Work. It is only when we start to apply them to our behavior and thought patterns that understanding takes place. If we know many concepts of the Work and never apply them to our lives, we have no understanding. On the other hand, we can have understanding by just knowing one concept and applying it. If we start to apply this concept in our lives (for example, complaining less), we will have a much greater understanding than the person who can spout off many of the concepts in the Work, but applies none of them to his life. Knowing and understanding are quite different things.

Requirements in the Work That Lead to Understanding

Before we can understand the Work, we must know the concepts it discusses. This can be obtained from reading books on the Work, going to groups that deal with the Work and having a guide or teacher who helps us learn the concepts. Gurdjieff and Ouspensky were both very insistent about the fact that we need a guide to do this Work. It is only those who get out of the bondage of life who are capable of leading others out. Unfortunately, I have no guide. Nicoll, however, did say that life can be our teacher if we non-identify with what happens to us, treating unpleasant things we meet equally with pleasant ones, thereby decreasing our mechanicalness and increasing our consciousness.

I attend a weekly study group where we read from and discuss the concepts of the Work, and I try to apply these concepts in my life—and every once in a while, I do succeed.

The second requirement is that we value the ideas of the Work. If we think it is a lot of nonsense, why would we make any effort to apply it? So, first the Work comes into our Intellectual Center. We hear the ideas. Then, if we value them, we start to spend more time studying them. We attend groups. We read books on it, and so on. If we claim we never have time to do the Work, then we are really not interested despite what we might say. It is like the man who claims he never has time to do the things his wife requests, but he always finds the time to read the horseracing sheet or, more likely today, to be on his computer. He apparently finds time for these activities. Where our interests are is where we spend our time.

After we get to know some of the ideas and they enter our Intellectual Center, we must value these Ideas so much that we get to love them. For Nicoll, there is little difference between love and value when taken in a practical way. For example, according to Nicoll, if we say we love a person and do not value that person, it is not love. When we begin to highly value the Work and therefore love it, the ideas of the Work enter our Emotional Center. The Emotional Center gives us the energy to apply the Work ideas rather than just be aware of them in our Intellectual Center.

However, as we discussed before, we all have various 'I's or personalities in us. Some 'I's think the Work is a lot of nonsense and want us to simply disregard it, but if we have some 'I's who see the value of the Work, they will form a Deputy Steward. This Deputy Steward will take charge of the various 'I's and even if it can't control all the various 'I's, it can control enough of them so that those 'I's who want to do the Work will find the time to do it.

Observing Ourselves: An Inside Job

Even if we value the Work, and have it in our Emotional Center, to think we can make big changes, such as never being negative again, is totally unrealistic. We may think we haven't been negative for a while, and then someone can make some comment, and we just explode in a sea of negativity. Our first task is just to observe ourselves. This is the start and basis of the Work. The bridge between hearing the ideas of the Work and changing our being is self-observation. By self-observation, we can chip away at little parts of ourselves after we have a "photograph" of how we really are by taking mental photos of ourselves in various situations and storing them away. The first thing to realize is that no one knows how he or she really behaves, although we can see it in others.

When I was a student at the University of Michigan, I had an English teacher, Alan Seager, who was also a novelist. He told the class he needed models for the characters in his novels and he often modeled them on people he knew. He would describe their behavior in very great detail. At first he thought one of his friends or colleagues would barge into his office and ask how he had the nerve to tell all the details in print. No one ever barged into Seager's office. At first that surprised Seager, but then he realized people do not see themselves as they are, but we—as observers—can see how other people behave. This is why some of us could write a Dear Abby column and give sound advice to others.

Someone loses or misplaces his wallet. We can tell him that there is nothing to worry about. All the credit cards have a $50 limit, and if he notifies the credit card company, there is no liability, and they will simply issue him another card. He can get a duplicate driver's license for a few dollars. All he really has lost is the cash in the wallet. It's easy for us to say that because it is not our wallet; we are not identified with it, and can be objective. When it is our wallet, we get identified with its loss, lose force, and completely forget ourselves. Some people will not become so upset when they misplace or lose their wallet. Other things, however, will upset them. Only by observing oneself can one see what one is really like and how one reacts to life. No one but us can observe and ultimately change us. It is an "inside job."

There is one other point I would like to make about observing other people's behavior and inferring from it their psychological state. This is also a tricky matter. We may think we know how others are because we can see how they behave, but we are only observing their external actions, not where they are living psychologically. If you want to read a great novel illustrating this point, I highly recommend *The Good Soldier* by Ford Maddox Ford. It is supposedly the only French novel written in the English language. It has nothing to do with conventional war, but describes two wealthy couples, one American and one English, traveling in Europe. What I learned from this novel is that we really don't know what is going on with people internally by observing their external circumstances.

What Changes Can We Make in the Beginning?

If we think we can make any big changes in our behavior, we will probably be very disappointed. At first, the things we can observe are some of our small habits. Let us suppose that before leaving home we have to look for our car keys or wallet or glasses or some other item that we use frequently and often misplace. We usually get flustered and may swear because we are in a rush, and frustrated because we can't find our keys. We have become frustrated on many occasions because of this.

The first thing we can do is to consciously try to change the situation so we will know where our keys and wallet always are. One way is to have a place where we always leave our wallet and car keys upon entering our home. The only things we put in this designated place are the keys and wallet. It could be a small basket by the door or a hook for our keys. We also make it a rule to place the keys and wallet there as soon as we enter our home. If we are consistent in applying this rule, there will be fewer times when we can't find our keys and wallet before leaving.

There will still be times, however, because we are unloading packages or the phone rings as we enter our house, when we do not place our keys and wallet in the designated place. Then when we leave and can't find our keys and/or wallet we become very frustrated and go into a negative state, often cursing and always losing force. We can think in a new way and realize we have not lost our keys and wallet and that they are in the house. We can have a spare set of keys and leave, or—if we keep looking—we can say to ourselves, "I have not lost the keys and wallet. They are here." We can do this whenever we have to look for them.

The Work suggests a four-step approach when we cannot find something. First, if we are in a negative state, we observe we are in a negative state, so we are becoming more conscious of our state and not taking ourselves for granted and assuming we are this negative state. Second, we observe our thoughts. What thoughts come to us when we have lost or misplaced something? Are we beating ourselves up, telling ourselves what a fool we are, or blaming others who did something to make us misplace or lose the item? Third, we notice the emotions we are in, especially the internal taste. Are we mad, and walking around in an angry mood? Or are we frustrated and in a mood of self-depreciation? Again, what is our taste like internally? Fourth, and finally, we notice our movements and our expressions, and take a mental photograph of them.

If we can do this without being self-critical, just be an impartial observer of our own activity, and repeat this process several times when we misplace or lose something, we are less likely to react mechanically. Eventually we can change how we react in this situation. As a person who has spent a significant part of his life looking for misplaced keys and other things, I have discovered that I have been able to change how I react when I misplace things today.

This is one of my successes caused by the Work. I realize this may seem like "small potatoes" compared to the big things we want to change in our lives, but we have to start somewhere, and the Work says we must start on small matters where we do have a chance to succeed. Gurdjieff used to say we should be able to keep our goals in our pockets, meaning they should be small enough so we can achieve them.

If we observe ourselves, we might also notice that we are often, if not continually in an internal considering mode, having thoughts about other people and how they have somehow "done us wrong" or owe us something. Sometimes we can stop this internal considering by simply telling ourselves to stop. To do this, we must be able to observe ourselves doing it. If we feel very intense about something and are totally in its grip, (for instance, feelings of jealousy), we probably can't stop it, but at least we can become aware of what we are doing.

Although these may seem like very small changes, it can take a lot of frustration out of our lives, and shows that change in small things is possible with the Work. Large changes are much more difficult because there is something in our character that keeps us going in a circle and not moving forward toward any change, and this is our Chief Feature.

Our Chief Feature

According to the Work, we all have a Chief Feature that controls our personality. It keeps us going around in the same circle.

We may try to make changes, but we always end up in the same place. There is a modern saying, "To do the same thing over and over again and expect a different result is a sign of insanity." From the Work point of view, a more appropriate saying would be, "Why do I keep doing different things and always end up with the same result?" It is our Chief Feature that keeps the results always coming out the same.

The Chief Feature is something the person must discover by observation. Other people can more easily see our chief feature. If, however, someone told it to us, we wouldn't believe it and would find it very hard to take. We would either say it's not true, or in some way justify our denial. The Chief Feature wants to remain in control of us and therefore will use any rationalization to keep itself in power. It is the axis around which our life pivots. It is very specific. For some it might be always finding fault. For some it might be making everything difficult, and for others it might be never being able to take orders or even suggestions from others.

Other people might be able to see our Chief Feature, but we cannot see our own without long observation of ourselves. We have to take many mental photographs of ourselves in many situations and finally we get glimpses of our Chief Feature that runs our life. Each time we take one of these mental photographs we are allowing some consciousness into our life. We will see our Chief Feature only when we have the power to endure it. We must have something to replace it, something we value - such as the Work - to increase our consciousness and the awakening of ourselves.

There is one other matter about the Chief Feature that should be pointed out. It ties in with a whole system of viewing how man reacts to the world called the Enneagram. Gurdjieff discussed many aspects of the Enneagram that he referred to as a moving diagram, reflecting all of the laws of the Work, including the Law of Three and the Law of Seven that will be discussed later. Although not part of the Work, a system of personality types developed from the Enneagram. Basically, there are nine approaches to handling our life. They are usually given names although the names vary somewhat by different authors. The viewpoints are as follows: 1. The Perfectionist; 2. The Giver; 3. The Performer (always doing); 4. The Tragic Romantic; 5. The Observer; 6. The Devil's Advocate (always expects the worst); 7. The Epicure; 8. The Boss; and 9. The Mediator. We each have our viewpoint and can go to other viewpoints to balance ourselves or to others when stressed. The relation of these nine points is discussed in Helen Palmer's *The Enneagram* as well as many other books.

We Are Under the Influence of Laws

The Work says we are all under the influence of laws. The lower we are in terms of the Work, the more laws we will be under. To take an example of ordinary life, someone who is incarcerated is under more laws than one who is not. Or take military life: the private is under more laws than the sergeant, who is under more laws than the lieutenant, who is under more laws than the colonel, who is under more laws than the general. The freer we get from identification and the other negative states we indulge ourselves in, the fewer laws we are under and therefore the freer we become. The ironic thing about the Work is that we have to place ourselves under more laws through the Work, so that eventually we will be under fewer laws in life. The Work talks about many laws. Two very important laws that we are all under are the Law of Three and the Law of Seven.

The Law of Three

This law is extremely important in the Work and has many subtle aspects. Basically, the Law of Three states that every manifestation in the universe is the result of three forces. The first is the active force, the second is the passive force, and the third is the neutralizing force. Unless we have all three of these forces, the event or manifestation will not occur. The first force can also be thought of as the initiating force, the second force as the resisting, and the third force as the connecting force or point of application. This idea of three forces is an ancient one. In Hinduism, for example, God is made up of three gods or forces: Brahma, the creator, Vishnu, the preserver and Shiva, the destroyer. Hindus worship all three, and life is the balance between these three forces.

Let us look at this law on an individual level. We are unemployed. We want a job. The desire for obtaining a job is the first or initiating force. The second force is that we dislike making all the necessary and persistent efforts that are required to obtain a job. This is the resisting force. If only these two forces are at work, nothing will happen. We want a job (the initiating force), but we don't want to go through the hassle that is necessary for looking for a job (resisting force), so we make no effort or only limited efforts to seek a job. If somehow we have a means of support and do not need the salary to live on, nothing is going to happen. We drift because the third force is not present. Let us suppose, however, we are overdue on our rent, behind in our car payments, and have little food. Then this condition becomes the third force that makes us go out and do what is necessary to find a job. The coming together or conjunction of these three forces constitutes a triad in the Work.

The three forces are creative only at the point of their conjunction and here we have a manifestation, a creation, and an event takes place. Without the third or connecting force nothing happens and from this connecting or third force another triad springs. One triad or train of events will produce another. The connecting force from the first triad becomes the active force in the second triad. The job obtained because of the need for money now becomes the active force or first force. For example, wanting to do well on the job is now the first force.

The second force or resistance is that we don't like the fact we have to work at night or perhaps we don't get along with our supervisor. Unless a third neutralizing force develops, we will stay exactly where we are. The neutralizing or third force might be realizing that we need the money to pay our back bills and therefore we put up with the night hours or the disliked supervisor and continue on the job. On the other hand, the neutralizing force might be that we are a musician and need our nights free for our music and therefore quit the job. In any event, the third or neutralizing force will then create another triad with it, becoming the active or first force.

Another way of looking at these forces is that the active or first force is what we want. The passive or second force can be taken as what resists or prevents what we want. Until we see the active and passive forces it is impossible to see the neutralizing force. According to the Work, a desire, a train of thought or an idea is not a thing, but a force. To understand how things manifest themselves in our lives, we have to realize that they all involve these three forces. If we desire something (first force), we should be aware that there is a resistance to obtaining it (second force). These forces work with individuals, but also with couples, groups and society itself. Every couple is familiar with the concept that if one partner suggests something, often the first thing out of their partner's mouth is the word, "No." They give resistance immediately.

The Work says that the only way we can understand these three forces is by practical study, not by theoretical discussions. We can do this by acting on ourselves to change something internally or to change how we react to external events. As far as acting on ourselves, let us suppose we want to struggle with a habit. Someone is a smoker and wishes to stop. The desire to stop is the active or first force. The passive or second force is the person's resistance to stopping. The person could start to observe when he starts to smoke a cigarette: what was the stimulation or event that led him to take it out of the pack and light it? What time of day does it happen? How did he feel immediately before and after smoking it?

By making these observations, a person might start to

understand his resistance. He never used to be aware of these things, and now he is becoming more conscious of why and when he starts to smoke. He still might not stop but he is raising his consciousness to the reasons he smokes. Until a neutralizing force comes, he will continue as he is, wanting to quit but not quitting. The neutralizing force might result in his quitting or in giving up his desire to quit. By struggling with his habit through self-observation he becomes more conscious of the forces involved.

As to internal events, let us say we are struggling with an expression of unpleasant emotions towards someone we dislike. The active or first force would be the desire not to express negative emotions toward that person. The passive or second force would be the resistance to this desire that results in expressing negative emotions toward this person. So, if we start to observe ourselves and see under what circumstances we express these negative emotions towards the disliked person, we will become more conscious of what we are doing. Even if we can't stop ourselves from expressing these negative emotions, just becoming aware of them is a big step forward. Eventually, if we continue observing ourselves, we might be able to refrain every now and then from expressing a negative emotion. By observing ourselves, we are becoming aware of the strength of the second (passive) resisting force.

A Shortcut to Decrease the Resisting Force:
"Will" What We Have to Do

According to the Work, there is one shortcut to decrease the second force and that is willing what we have to do. Suppose we have to write a report. If we will it and go to it with enthusiasm, the second force will be greatly reduced, and we will get the report finished much faster than if we drag ourselves to the task. The question is always whether we are doing something with enthusiasm or just dragging ourselves to the task because we really don't want to do it. Nicoll relates a time he was with Carl Jung, the psychoanalyst. Jung had to give a lecture on a subject he didn't think his audience would be interested in. After discussing it with Nicoll, Jung said, "Let's go to it!" and with enthusiasm went and gave the lecture. Those things we do with enthusiasm and a "Let's go to it!" attitude will be a lot easier than those tasks to which we drag ourselves because we really don't want to do them.

When we do the task only because some form of third force is intervening (e.g., we will fail the class if the paper isn't handed in by a certain date), we will always have a high degree of resistance or second force because we are not willing to do the task. This latter condition is so strong in our society that there is a saying that if it weren't for the last minute, nothing would get done. Obviously, for most of us those things we like, such as playing golf, we will do with a lot more enthusiasm than say mowing the lawn, which most of us resist as long as possible. We all have also noticed that those things we resisted because we didn't will to do them but finally had to do them were often not as bad nor took as long as our dreaded anticipation. The dishes took just a few minutes to wash, and the lawn was mowed in twenty minutes.

If we had willed doing the dishes, mowing the lawn, writing the paper, we could have done them much faster because there would have been less resistance to doing them. On the other hand, every time we become negative about something, this increases the resistance to start the task, and it will take us a longer time to complete it.

Nothing will change until the third force enters and a conjunction takes place between the first and second force, but if we will what we have to do, we cut down on the magnitude of the second force. It should be noted, however, that there is no way to completely eliminate second force, whether it be in our external goals, such as seeking a home, or in our personal goals, such as complaining less. In fact, life would lose interest if anything we wanted would be instantly produced without any effort to overcome resistances. The poor little rich boy who gets everything he wants without any effort on his part becomes a spoiled bored brat. We truly appreciate what we have to make efforts to obtain.

The quality of the third force will be crucial in what the final manifestation or event will be in any situation. From the Work standpoint, the change in the quality of the neutralizing force will change not only the relation of forces in a triad, but may reverse the active and passive forces.

The Three Forces in Relationship to Essence and Personality

As stated earlier, according to the Work, essence is what we are born with and comes from Higher Powers, while personality is what we acquire in life by imitating others around us. When life is the neutralizing force, personality is active and essence is passive. When the Work becomes the neutralizing or third force, the positions of personality and essence are reversed, with essence becoming active and personality passive.

In general, if we observe our Personality, we will find certain characteristics such as being argumentative, angry, stingy, and so on. The first step in changing our Personality is to dislike the way it is acting. If we justify the way Personality is behaving, we will then never make the necessary effort to change the particular trait we have observed.

Let us take the example of our struggling with an expression of unpleasant emotions toward a person we dislike. If we are struggling with this and are students of the Work, we start uncritically observing ourselves when we make these negative expressions. We might see that we always lose force after making them or that making them gives us a bad taste in our mouth. After much effort and many failures, occasionally when in the company of this person we consciously refrain from expressing a negative emotion toward him. In addition, when in the company of others who are also expressing negative emotions toward this individual, we make the conscious decision to withhold our criticism or negative emotion toward this person.

At first, we might feel weak because we are not acting in our customary way. We are giving something up, a bit of our personality. Then, however, we might notice that we feel better about ourselves in a subtle way, have a better taste in our mouth, and have gained some force by not expressing the negative emotions. Others might think we are becoming dull because we are not so quick to join the gossip and are quieter now. What is happening is that by employing the Work as our neutralizing or third force, there is a change going on in our essence. Our being is undergoing some change. This will take a long time to achieve. It is not an easy task, as anyone who has tried not to express his negative emotions has found out. We all have negative emotions.

On the other hand, if life is the neutralizing or third force, we will continue to express negative emotions toward the person we dislike. We make justifications because we think we are right in this particular instance. Thus, we continue to express these emotions, and nothing will change. Our personality will be active and our essence passive. Our life, therefore, will go on exactly as before.

The Work also states that not only have we acquired a personality, but we also have acquired all sorts of opinions and attitudes. We were born into a family of Democrats so we usually become Democrats. We are Republicans if we were born into a family of Republicans. We assume our opinions and attitudes were all thought out when actually they were just acquired automatically. We become completely identified with our opinions and attitudes just as we identify with our personalities. The Work suggests we try to argue the other side of our opinions just to show how another side of the issue is possible.

We should take none of this on faith or, for that matter, anything else in this book. The only things the Work wants us to believe in are what we understand for ourselves, and the Work says we can obtain this by observing ourselves. How do we act? We must become aware of how we act. There is no substitute for self-observation. It is the main tool of the Work. If we can start to observe the active first force and the passive second force within us, it will throw a great deal of light on why we often don't accomplish our goals. It should be pointed out that essence and personality are under two different laws.

The Laws of Accident and Fate
in Relationship to Essence and Personality

Essence is real. It is what really belongs to us. Personality is unreal, and although it is necessary to develop to get on in the world, it is not really our true self. Whether we are under the Law of Accident or Law of Fate depends upon where we place our feeling of ourselves. If our feeling of ourselves comes from life (influences from A), then we will be under the Law of Accident.

Influences such as money, fame, prestige, and the numerous other influences come from life. If, for example, we place our sense of self in the amount of money we have and our stocks go down substantially, we would feel very bad—and some in fact have committed suicide over the loss of their money. Others might place their sense of self in their fame or social climbing, belonging to the right set or getting invited to the right party. While everything is going well these people are happy, but once "the phone stops ringing" and the writer isn't called to write more screenplays or the actor to play more parts, or the party invitations stop coming, these people feel terrible. Others place their sense of self in their children and try to live their lives through their offspring. When things go well they feel good, but when their children disappoint them, they feel terrible.

In all these situations the sense of self is outside the person; we cannot control the rise and fall of the stock market; we cannot control whether the phone will ring offering us some employment or invitation, or if our children in the end will not do everything or anything we want, so we feel bad. Since the sense of self is outside ourselves, anything can happen, and therefore the Work says we are under the Law of Accident.

When we get into the Work and have an intermediary to screen us from having the events of life swamp us, then we start to develop our essence and we are no longer under the Law of Accident, but the Law of Fate. We are following our own destiny and are not bowled over by every rise or fall of the stock market, or whether the phone rings, or what our children do. It is not that we don't care, but our sense of self is no longer completely tied up by the external events because we are developing our own inner direction and developing our essence. We will be acting out our fate. This doesn't necessarily mean that only "good" things will happen to us. If, for example, our fate is to be an airplane pilot, we might have an accident that kills us. But we were acting in a way that came from our essence.

On the other hand, if we are acting from personality, anything can happen to us. It doesn't matter how hard we work at things; if they are controlled by our personality we are open to more accidents happening to us. Say a young woman is pressured by her family rather than by her own inner drive to become an attorney. She doesn't really like the law but loves growing things and working in gardens. By going to law school and doing the three years of hard work, she earns her law degree and then studies intensely to pass the bar exam. This woman, however, is not rewarded for all her efforts in the true sense. For example, after seven years in college and law school, she ends up with a firm in a large city building where no windows can be opened, and there is no fresh air in the building. She then must work extremely long hours as a young attorney to work herself up in the firm. Anything could happen to this woman; she is under more laws because she is following her personality rather than her essence. With this woman, for example, she has climbed the long ladder to success and finally can look over the wall, but she discovers that she has been on the wrong ladder. If her career had been connected to gardening in some form, she would have followed her true calling or essence, and would have been subject to fewer laws because she was doing what her nature called for. For another woman, it might be that becoming a lawyer was what her essence brought her to.

It is always interesting to me when one meets a very young person who knows exactly what he wants to be when he grows up. It could be argued that his family planted ideas in his head, and it is not his own true essence. Quite often, however, the choice is not anything the family encouraged, but one they might even have disparaged. Others, at some time in their lives see a potential occupation for the first time and know that this is it for them. I have heard of several accounts of students at school who took their first acting class or performing in their first play and felt, "This is it!" Acting is all they ever want to do from then on.

I know a man who, after leaving the army after the Second World War, walked by a body shop. He looked into the window watching the men work on cars and thought, "This is what I want to do." He went to a technical school to learn body work and did that for his entire working career. I brought several cars to him to be fixed over the years and referred many friends and clients to him. The man loved his work. Such people, once they choose their career, never even think of another possibility.

I once attended a seminar by Alan Watts in San Francisco. He said that good dancers never think which foot is going to go next. Only bad dancers do that. Watts said that real freedom was not freedom of choice but freedom from choice. These people are following a deep calling or essence. When they make their decision they know they have made the right decision.

Another way of viewing these two laws is as Joseph Campbell's idea of following your bliss. He said that when we are doing what we love to do, regardless of financial considerations or external pressures, we will be happy. When we do things for some external reason, such as thinking a career will provide us with financial security or prestige, we are following personality—and usually our false personality. It turns out that those who follow their bliss are usually happier than those who do things for external reasons that don't feel right.

As Arnold M. Patent points out in his book, *You Can Have It*

All, when we do what we love, it is an expression of our talent. Talent and creativity are gifts given to us as an expression of the abundance of the universe. As to our health, Balzac points out, "A man's health seldom suffers from the work he loves and does for its own sake." The fact is that most of us are living under the Law of Accident rather than the Law of Fate. As Henry David Thoreau said in his classic *Walden* written in 1854, "The mass of men lead lives of quiet desperation"— and nothing much has changed since then. The purpose of the Work and all other forms of transformation is to turn our lives around, to make us think differently, to change us, and end the desperation so many of us feel. Why change is so difficult is partially explained by the Law of Seven.

The Law of Seven

The Law of Seven is also called the Law of Octaves and the Law of Scale. In life many things turn out very differently from what we intended. To paraphrase the words of the Scottish poet Robert Burns, the best laid plans of mice and men often go astray. When things do not go according to our expectations, the Work says this happens for two reasons: deviation of forces and retardation of forces.

As to deviation of forces, let us take a simple example. (I realize that this example may seem farfetched considering the frenetic lives most people live today, but let us assume, for the sake of illustration, it happened many years ago in a small town where the pace of life was much more leisurely and friendly.) John needs to mail a letter on a Saturday morning. He lives close to his post office and decides to walk there. On his way to the post office, he runs into a friend who he hasn't seen for a while, and the friend suggests they stop at a coffee shop so they can talk. While there, a few other mutual friends appear, and they all sit and chat together. Then someone suggests they go to a nearby restaurant and have lunch together. Since John is having such a good time talking with old friends he goes to lunch with them. After lunch, one of them suggests they all watch the football game at his house. John agrees. He goes there and has a couple of beers while watching the game. When the game is over, he decides it is time to go home. Upon arriving home, he takes his jacket off and notices that the letter is still in his jacket pocket. The mail has already gone out, and he will have to wait until Monday to mail it, so John has made a full circle without accomplishing his goal of mailing his letter—or perhaps John puts his hand in his pocket and realizes the letter is not there. He has lost it. We all have left our house with the intention of doing something, but we somehow got sidetracked and came home without accomplishing it. This is deviation of forces.

As to retardation of forces, have you ever been in someone's house that he built himself and noticed that all or some of the trim or other work still wasn't completed? Some people live in houses for years or maybe their entire lives without completely finishing them. How many people worked for a Master's or Ph.D. and did everything but write their dissertation? Years later, they still haven't completed it.

How many people say they will write a book? Most don't even start, but of those who do, how many people stop writing somewhere along the line, and the project never gets completed? How many people make a New Year's resolution that they are going to exercise regularly, and after a few months their exercise programs slowly wither? Many people have all sorts of projects in various stages of incompleteness. The people who started these projects are not lazy people. They had every intention of finishing them when they started out, but somehow the goal was never reached.

The Law of Seven explains why this happens. It uses the analogy of the musical scale. A musical scale is an ascending or descending series of tones preceded by a specified scheme of intervals and varying in pitch and interval size. It consists of seven notes, with the note "do" appearing at the beginning and "do" at the end. That is why it is also called the Law of Octaves. The notes are: do re mi fa sol la si do. They can be played in ascending or descending order. For those who understand anything about music, it is generally known that there is one semitone between each pair of notes, with the exception of the intervals mi-fa and si-do, with no intermediate semitone. On a piano, the black notes represent intermediate semitones, or half steps, between notes. Perhaps a more accurate way of viewing the scale is that there are really no gaps in the scale, only whole and half steps.

The important point in a beginning guide to this teaching is to have an understanding of what this scale and gaps or half steps between the notes mean. Everything starts straight, but then at the gap things start to veer in another direction because of the gap. According to the Work, this is why there are no straight lines in nature. Everything is continually veering off in another direction. In nature, what we see are circles and spirals, not straight lines.

How does the Law of Seven affect us? Let us suppose that the same John as in our earlier example has left his house on that Saturday morning to mail his letter when he met his friend who suggests they stop at a coffeehouse. This is the gap. If John does not exert extra effort here, he may very well get sidetracked from mailing his letter. What does it take to bridge the gap? According to the Work, it takes a shock or extra effort.

The first conscious shock in the Work is to remember oneself, to keep John from becoming identified with his friend and losing sight of his aim. If John can get the shock and remember himself and know what his goal is, he could say to his friend, "I'd like to, but I have to mail this letter. Would you like to walk with me to the post office so I can mail it and then we can go for some coffee?" His friend probably would have gone with him. If not, John would still keep to his purpose. At the point of the gap, we need a shock to jump the gap and continue to pursue our goal. Although I realize that mailing a letter is a quite mundane example, do not underestimate the importance of the conscious shock in order to jump this gap and keep oneself on the right track.

How many teachers have taken a child who was floundering and with the teacher's encouragement and belief in the student thus became the shock that caused that child to cross the gap and get his education or begin his career rather than veering off and dropping out of school? It could be argued that behind every man or woman's accomplishments there was a mother, father, or other adult who encouraged that child at a very young age to believe in himself, and thus either gave him the shocks as he went along or inculcated the confidence in him so he would be able to give himself the necessary shocks when the gaps appeared.

Those who were not given the shocks or encouragement from others must learn to develop their own shocks, whether it be early or later on in life, or they will not accomplish their goals. According to the Work, we do this by self-remembering. The first step in self-remembering is to start observing ourselves. No one can do this for us and, despite any encouragement we did get from parents or teachers for earlier shocks, we have to learn to give ourselves our own conscious shocks as we go through life.

One way of thinking about these gaps is that they are the resistances of the second force of the Law of Three. Unless these resistances can be overcome, we veer from our course, or the progress toward our goal slows down. Anyone who has taken on any involved project such as building a house, writing a book, or organizing a campaign for some cause knows that somewhere within sight of the goal things start to slow down. We need some type of shock to finish the project. If we don't supply it, the house, the manuscript, or the campaign never gets completed. These gaps exist in all the things we want to accomplish. According to the Work, each note on the scale itself can be broken down into the eight notes with the gaps. In order to get any project done correctly, each step must be done properly. If the foundation of the house is not square and level, there will be problems putting up the walls. It is necessary for each step to be accomplished correctly for the project to be successfully completed, and that will include the conscious shocks necessary along the way.

As to the ascending and descending nature of the scales themselves, the Work says we can look at them as levels. Everything happening is either ascending or descending. It does not stay on the same level for long. Good marriages get better as time goes on, and bad ones get worse with the passage of time. We may think we are on the same level, but we often can't see the subtle changes that raise or lower our level.

As to problem solving, nothing can be solved on the same level as the problem. We must go to a different, higher level to solve it. Two people in a marriage may feel animosity toward each other. At that level, they can't solve their problems. If they rise to a higher level because they love their children very much and want the best for them, they might be able to resolve their differences and form an amicable relationship whether they stay together or separate. Many couples with children have found that, after they have separated, they become good friends because of the mutual connection with their children, and they get along much better than when they were married. Of course, this doesn't happen in all cases, but the principle that we must solve our problems on a higher level applies.

The Work says that these two laws, the Law of Three and the Law of Seven, govern our lives. Since the purpose of the Work is to increase our consciousness and awaken us, we must start observing ourselves to see how these two laws apply in our lives. What we must learn is how to give ourselves conscious shocks.

How Do We Give Ourselves Conscious Shocks?

The question arises as to how we give ourselves the conscious shocks necessary to remember ourselves and get past these gaps in the scale. The Work says we need a teacher and a group. We cannot do it ourselves. We need a teacher and group because we are always falling asleep by either becoming identified with whatever we are doing or by external events that enter our lives. The Work uses all kinds of devices in groups and individual work to wake us up. For instance, every hour an alarm clock would go off as a signal for us to awaken and remember ourselves. Gurdjieff used to do the Stop exercise discussed earlier.

On a more mundane level, every time we start reading a book connected with the Work, it is an awakening call where we start to see how we have been asleep, and occasionally we will read something that will really shock us into awakening. I did this the other day when I read from Maurice Nicoll's book, *Psychological Commentaries on the Teachings of Gurdjieff and Ouspensky*, which discusses our attitude toward life. Nicoll's position is that it is best to think that the experiences we have are necessary for us. If we *don't* think this way, we will be continually making accounts and complaining that life is not fair. Only in this way do our experiences have more meaning to us, and this is the only way to gain something from life. We need each experience for our development, and rather than thinking that these occurrences are interruptions in our lives, they are exactly the experience we need at this point in our lives. In order to have this attitude, we must remember ourselves.

Reading about this was a shock to me. I was going to leave that night to see a specialist in another city for a medical consultation. I wondered why this was happening to me. When I read Nicoll's book, I realized that this was what I had to work on. It was not some interruption in my life, but my life itself, and I had to practice the principles of the Work. I had completely identified with my medical condition. After reading this passage, I realized this was a situation I had to nonidentify with. I felt much better after reading this. Subsequently, I came across Gurdjieff's remark, "Events are not against us." And in any situation, Gurdjieff said, we should ask ourselves, "What is good about it?"

As to the possibility of avoiding any unpleasant experiences, Nicoll discussed the idea that we cannot avoid all experiences that are unpleasant. If we have the money and opportunity to do so, there will not be any development in the Self. His idea was that if we never experienced any unpleasant experiences, we would probably grow more and more narrow and selfish, which always seems to happen when there is no development.

This was another shock to me, which made me conscious of the fact that there will always be some unpleasant experiences in my life that are the material I must work on to develop. When reading Nicoll and others in the Work, I often do not get any shocks or insights, but the knowledge is accumulative and continually develops a whole body of knowledge. Then every once in a while there is a shock from it, as it goes from the mere knowledge in the Intellectual Center into the heart or Emotional Center, and I know intuitively that what I read is true and it affects my life.

The key the Work stresses is that we must not only have knowledge of the Work but also apply it to our lives. What goes for reading applies even more when we attend meetings concerning the Work. If we go to a meeting regularly each week, each meeting is a shock that helps us to be more conscious of the Work.

The meetings might have all types of participants from people who have been participants for years to people who are there for the first time. The one common characteristic I have found in the few groups I have attended is the sincerity of the people who attend. Each group will be different, depending on its leader. Each leader may have very different techniques on how he wants to get the ideas of the Work across to his students and check if the ideas are actually applied. For example, when I attended Richard Liebow's group in San Francisco, one of the regular activities of the group was to have each student report on the effects of the teachings on his or her life during the past week, citing a specific example, including the day and time it occurred.

The group I started in 1997 now consists of five people. When I decided to have a local group in my hometown after coming back from my friend's meeting in San Francisco, I put up some signs around town, and placed a listing in an alternative weekly. A few people called and I met with one person, with the unusual name Christ Michael. I didn't think we had much in common, but he said, "At least we are both interested in the Work, so why don't we try?" I asked him if he would be willing to read Ouspensky's *In Search for the Miraculous*. He agreed. For a while we met at coffeehouses but ended up at my home. We read out loud, each taking turns, and asked questions or discussed what the text meant, or we cross-referenced certain points. We finished that book and read one by E. J. Gold, an author Christ Michael suggested.

We then started reading Ouspensky's book, *The Psychology of Man's Possible Evolution*, but when a new member, Elaine, joined our group, she suggested we read instead Maurice Nicoll's *Psychological Commentaries on the Teachings of Gurdjieff and Ouspensky*. This is a five-volume set that transcribes the talks that Nicoll gave in England mostly during the Second World War. Christ Michael had photocopied a chapter on a particular point. I was extremely impressed with this chapter, and so when it was suggested we switch to reading him, we were all willing to do so. We started reading Nicoll and have been reading him since December 1998. Christ Michael dropped out about six months after the three of us met together, and then the group consisted of only Elaine and me for over a year. In 2000, Kelley joined our group, and in 2001 Sharon joined. In 2002, Jeannie joined.

We have an ongoing listing about our group in an alternative monthly newspaper. Several people responded, and a few showed up for one or two meetings. We meet for about an hour and a half each week. We always start and end by saying our invocation, which is, "Whatever be the highest perfection of the human mind, may we realize it, simply by pausing frequently to focus inward to picture an image of an impartial observer/listener/experiencer/witness within ourselves." This is the invocation that Richard Liebow's group used in San Francisco to start and end their meetings and we adopted it for ours, as well. Then I add, "We have a right not to be negative. We can think in new ways. We can will the Work. We realize we are self developing beings who must make conscious efforts against the circumstances of our lives, so we do not become negative. And when in trouble ask, Am I a student of Gurdjieff?"

Incidentally, I have found that as I repeat this every day to myself as well as with the group, it is starting to have an effect on me. When, for example, I was in my tent on a camping trip and the zipper of my sleeping bag was not attached, so it could not be zippered up, at first I was very frustrated, but then I asked myself the question, Am I a student of Gurdjieff? and I calmed down and fixed the zipper myself. In the past I, would ask someone for help and they would do it for me. I am doing this in many situations that before would frustrate me and cause me to seek help from others. From my experience, I think these affirmations have to be said many hundreds, if not thousands of times, before they sink into our deep consciousness and to have an effect on our behavior. In the past I think I gave up on them much too quickly.

We start and end the meetings with the above words. Then, we ask each other in what way, if any, we have applied the Work to our lives this week. We then read from the book, interrupting if anyone reads some word incorrectly or to make comments or ask questions whenever we think it is appropriate. This may not sound like much, but each meeting and the topics read and discussed create a little shock that keeps us in the Work. Because of out of town trips of various members, we sometimes need to change the day and time of the meeting, but we always meet.

In addition to my weekly group meetings, I try to read one chapter of Nicoll each day. Each chapter is a talk and is only a few pages long, yet I feel that reading a chapter a day is a way I give myself a daily shock to stay with the Work. Sometimes I think I am not making any progress, but that is those 'I's in me that want to give up; another group of 'I's in me realizes the importance of the Work and keeps me reading. There are occasions where I realize I haven't expressed a negative emotion, or I have acted in a new way to external impressions or have pulled out of a bad mood or event faster than I used to. At other times I become mired in negative states and totally identified with the external events that life is handing me. The Law of the Pendulum explains these mood swings.

The Law of the Pendulum

We are all under the Law of the Pendulum and so is nature. Everything changes. Winter follows summer, day follows night. Our hearts rest and then they contract. The Bible says it best:

To everything there is a season and a time to every purpose under the heaven, a time to be born and a time to die, a time to plant and a time to pluck up that which is planted, a time to kill and a time to heal, a time to break down and a time to build up, a time to weep and a time to laugh, a time to mourn and a time to dance, a time to cast away stones and a time to gather stones together, a time

107

to embrace and a time to refrain from embracing, a time to see and a time to lose, a time to keep and a time to cast away, a time to rend and a time to sew, a time to keep silence and a time to speak, a time to love and a time to hate; a time for war, and a time for peace. (Ecclesiastes III 1-8)

The problem in life is that we often don't see the connection between the opposite swings of the pendulum. Moreover, the swings are of different lengths, and they swing at different speeds. The length of the pendulum from birth to death is much longer than from enthusiasm to dejection. Everything changes, and we can be in the same place in the pendulum swing but be going toward opposite poles. For example, we can be pleasant as we head toward the irritable pole or the peaceful pole. The problem is when we get caught on either pole and do not realize change will happen and we may soon be at the other pole.

The Work says that if we identify with one side of the pole, we will also become identified with the other side of the pendulum and our life will be nothing but ups and downs with little peace. The Work points out that there is a center point in the swing, an equilibrium or balance point, before the pendulum begins swinging over in the other direction. In this point of balance is where peace can be found. The only way we can do that is not to identify with either pole. The middle point is the Way of Tao, the middle path of Buddha. It is the point where the Work says we remember ourselves. This then becomes the third force (the neutralizing force), and here is where we can change the level of our being by staying in the balance point.

What we all do is identify with either end of the pendulum swing—love or hate, success or failure. When we are at one end or the other, we do not realize we will not stay there indefinitely. Everything changes, not only people but also the properties of things. Something that works well for a while will not work well and may even harm us at some point. We want things to remain fixed. If we are on the end of the swing of the pendulum that we like, such as being in love, or successful, or famous, or healthy, or enthusiastic, we would like to have this position frozen so that nothing changes, and we will stay there forever. Things in our life will no more stay the same than thinking summer will last forever. Fall will come soon enough and then winter.

In the physical world we are usually willing to accept that the seasons change and night will follow day. Even in the physical world we find it hard to accept that the TV, refrigerator, stereo, and car will eventually not operate as well as they once did and maybe even stop running altogether. We want them to run well forever. In our personal lives, we get very upset when things don't go the way we want them to. When we are in love, we want this love to go on forever just as we first experienced it and are shocked when its nature changes. We expect the stock market to go up forever and are shocked when it starts to fall. We are devastated when our child, whom we love so much, and whom we thought loved us in return, can't wait to get away from us.

The Work says we become unhappy because we identify with one extreme of the pendulum and then we identify with the other when it swings over. To become balanced is to realize that everything changes and that we can see both sides of the swing. We try to get to the middle, the still point, where the pendulum is in neutral before it starts swinging in the other direction. We do this by taking small steps. One of the key precepts of Greek philosophy was "Know thyself." We are usually unaware that the other key precept was "Moderation is all things." Living a life of moderation will help us from going from one extreme swing of the pendulum to the other. It isn't easy to do this and takes lots of practice. It isn't easy for most of us to stop eating before we feel totally full. If we could learn to do this, we would feel and look better and be healthier. Eating in moderation to live rather than living to eat in excess will produce a very different result from our present condition. The same holds true in all areas of life. Bernard Baruch, the Wall Street whiz of years ago, warned against being too greedy and trying to squeeze out the last dollar of profit. It is not realistic to expect to buy in at the very bottom or sell at the very top. Exercise is good for us but if we do it in excess we can easily injure ourselves, as many have found out.

Life lived in the ordinary way and ruled by the Law of the Pendulum is a life full of extreme swings and ups and downs: victory to defeat; success to failure, jealousy to triumph, love to hate, fame to anonymity and so on forever. The Work says life is insoluble. There is no peace to be found there. It can only be found by looking at life through the Work, not by looking at the Work through life. If we realize that an unpleasant experience is exactly what we need at this moment in our lives to practice the principles of the Work, namely nonidentifying, then we do not need to resent what is happening to us. We can realize this is exactly what we need at this particular moment in our life to work on. If we can remain balanced internally despite what is happening in our lives externally, our life experiences become very valuable as teaching tools. We then can take each of life's experiences and use them for school work to practice not being negative in these particular circumstances. This takes conscious effort. It builds internal strength.

If, on the other hand, we view the Work through life, it is just some abstract concepts, and our happiness or unhappiness will be dependent on what external events are happening in our lives. Since the only constant is change, the pendulum will always be swinging from one side to the other. Our lives will be a continual up and down, sometimes feeling good and sometimes bad, but never bringing us any balance or peace.

The Work says that while everything appears to swing back and forth and the Law of the Pendulum is a very practical way of analyzing the extremes we go through them, actually, things go around in a circle. So if we can stay in a nonidentified state by remembering ourselves, we will realize that "this too will pass" when things we don't like are happening to us, as well as when things we like are happening.

The Fourth Way

The way of the Work is called the Fourth Way because we use the external events of life as the material to work on rather than as events to avoid. The name of the Fourth Way was arrived at by comparing it with three other ways: the fakir who uses his will to control his body; the monk who uses his will to control his emotions; and the yogi who uses his will to control his mind. With these methods, the student sometimes goes to a monastery or some type of sanctuary to meditate and study, removing himself from his ordinary life. There the student goes inward into himself in meditation for long periods of time, whether it is one day, one week, a few months, or the rest of his life. These methods work for some people, but many find after they leave the sanctuary, which most do, or after completing their meditation period and entering ordinary life again, their problems come back and they are in the same place internally as they were before. Most people do not leave their normal lives to go to a sanctuary or set aside a portion of their day to meditate or partake in some spiritual practice.

In the Fourth Way, we do not try to get away from our present circumstances for a long period or even short periods; instead, we use them as the material to transform ourselves. If we are constant worriers, then we work on nonidentifying with worrying. It is not easy. Development comes slowly, but if we can stop being a worrier or reduce the time we worry, we will have made a significant change in our lives that will affect our level of being. One will become a different type of person. On the other hand, if we happen to be worriers and go off to a monastery to find ourselves, we will find lots to worry about, even in a monastery, perhaps even more than we found outside.

There are other ways in which the Fourth Way differs. The principal requirement of the Fourth Way is understanding. The Work says a man should do nothing that he does not understand except as an experiment under the guidance of a teacher. The more we understand, the greater will be the results of our efforts. An important thing to realize about understanding is that it grows as we grow. The higher our level of being, the deeper we will understand things. Work ideas that we thought we understood will take on new meanings. Whereas before we saw only one meaning, as our understanding increases, we may see many and much deeper ones. For example, when we first read parables in the Gospels we have a certain understanding of them, but as our being develops we will understand them at deeper levels. In short, the Gospels will develop in meaning as we develop in being.

The Fourth Way asks us to take nothing on faith. We must see for ourselves the truth of what the Work teaches. For example, when the Work says we are machines, always reacting in the same ways to external events, the Work doesn't want us to just accept this idea on faith. It wants us to observe ourselves and see for ourselves that we do continually react in the same way to external events. Unless we see for ourselves, we should not accept this idea. Nicoll says it takes one to two years of self-observation to realize we are machines. Until we are satisfied that this is true for us, we should not do anything about it based on mere faith. The Fourth Way asks us to continually verify ideas and methods and take nothing for granted.

If we do understand by observing ourselves that we are machines because we cannot help doing what we do, and everything happens in the only way it could happen, then we are able to forgive. It is no one's fault, as it could not have happened differently. One test of our level of being is our ability to forgive. Those of us who go around with all sorts of grudges and resentments against others for what they did or did not do represent a very low level of being. Anyone who has been around such a person knows how heavy it is to be around him.

On the other hand, to learn to forgive raises our level of being because we realize that whatever we see in the other person is at least partially in us. The highest level of being and forgiveness is Christ who, when on the cross, said: "Father forgive them for they know not what they do." Many of us think forgiveness is only about forgiving other people's actions. Since most everyone is his or her own worst critic, learning to forgive ourselves is where the real work on forgiveness must begin. Once we learn to forgive ourselves, learning to forgive others is "child's play."

The Fourth Way is sometimes referred to as "The Way of the Sly Man." There are several aspects to this concept. The most important one is that the Sly Man is a clever man or woman. He has discovered that he does not need to go to a temple or retreat or set aside a certain period of the day to meditate. Not that any of these are bad, and they in fact have helped many people, but the Sly Man has realized wherever he is at any time of day, the Work is there for him to do if he is interested in pursuing it.

The Fourth Way is a modern 24/7 technique. It is not that we apply it every minute, but the Sly Man knows it is always available. We can walk into a store and make a pleasant comment to the sales clerk who has probably been standing on his feet for several hours, and we lift his spirits. We can give our thanks to people who do things for us. These latter events are examples of how we can practice external considering all day long. When we are frustrated by having to wait in line or are caught in a traffic jam, we can practice observing our impatience and/or anger and how upset we are. Wherever we are, there is the Work.

The efforts we make in the Work should be a private affair. Our efforts are not to be broadcast to others for the sake of showing what great progress we are making. For example, "You know, Shirley, I haven't complained about you for the last twenty minutes." When we broadcast our efforts concerning the Work, these efforts become part of our False Personality—we want praise for our efforts, and it is that very desire for praise that makes them not true Work efforts.

There is another aspect of the Sly Man and that is the pill he or she has discovered. When the Sly Man observes himself and sees some aspect of himself that is not quite right or some action that is not laudatory, rather than defending himself, blaming others or justifying himself, the Sly Man swallows the pill, accepting the fact that it is something in him that is at fault and does not blame others.

Gurdjieff described another aspect of the pill as that the Sly Man's Pill is self-remembering in different ways at different times, according to the situation. The Sly Man can remember himself anywhere. He has the ability to turn himself around. When we are identified, the problem is that things stick to us. We can't get free of them. The Sly Man's Pill allows him to remember himself no matter what the circumstances and free himself from a particular identification.

There are schools that teach the Fourth Way, but I believe the Fourth Way involves becoming a more balanced person, and the first step is self-observation. As to teachers of the Fourth Way, I would think the one criterion of all successful educators of the Work is that they are balanced men or women who have reached the level of man number four on Gurdjieff's hierarchy of development.

The Seven Levels of Man

There is a specific language to the Work. Gurdjieff was adamant in his feeling that people do not understand each other because they give different meanings to the same words and, thus, people cannot accurately communicate with each other. Gurdjieff has very specific categories for many things. We will discuss the categories regarding the classification of people. He bracketed them into three divisions. The first three classifications of men are all in the same category, called the Circle of Mechanical Humanity. They are men in whom one center mainly dominates: in man number one, it is the Instinctive-Moving Center; in man number two, it is the Emotional Center; and in man number three, it is the Intellectual Center.

No one uses just one center, but because of the domination of one center, each sees things differently according to which center he is dominated by. This Circle of Mechanical Humanity is characterized by misunderstanding between people because they do not understand themselves or other people and are prone to violence. It is also referred to in the Work as the circle of "confusion of tongues" or Babel, where misunderstandings, quarrels, strife, conflict, violence and war keep recurring. These three levels, because of their "one-sidedness," lack balance and are easily knocked off base by nearly anything that goes against their wishes (including things like the weather). Because of this, they are usually in negative moods, which often lead to violence.

Man number four forms the Intermediate Circle. The main characterization of this man is that he has achieved balance in his life and so is called the "balanced man." He uses all his centers and nothing can throw him off base. He is beginning to understand others and begins to overcome the violence in himself. This is a distinct step up from man one, two, or three. A number four man has much greater unity than man one, two or three. The number of different 'I's in him has decreased. In general, as we develop in the Work, the number of 'I's in us shrinks, and we are headed in the direction of our Real 'I', which is just one, rather than many.

Men of numbers five, six, and seven form the Conscious Circle of Humanity. These are men or women who understand each other. They have freed themselves of violence and have developed themselves in all the lower centers (the Instinctive-Moving, Emotional and Intellectual). They also have the power of being conscious from a lesser to a greater extent in the Higher Emotional and Higher Mental Centers. These higher centers are our guides, but man one, two and three have too much static in their lives in the form of negative states to hear them. The Higher Emotional and Mental Centers transmit influences that man one, two and three cannot hear.

It is from the Circle of Conscious Humanity that B influences originate. They originate as C influences, but become changed and altered in various ways when they come in contact with mechanical life and become B influences. This is why the Gospels, for example, are B influences. They were written many years after Christ had died. Paul and his student Luke, for example, never heard Christ speak. C influences can be transmitted orally only from one who understands to one who is beginning to understand. This is how the great masters transmitted their teachings orally to their students, whether they were Jesus, Buddha, Mohammed, or the modern masters, Ramakrishna and Yogananda.

The aim of the Work for man one, two and three is to become a "balanced man," to become man number four. Only by overcoming all our weaknesses so that we can use all our centers and not be thrown off base can we do this. This takes tremendous effort. First we have to observe ourselves to see what our weaknesses are and then strive to overcome them. If we try to justify our weaknesses rather than making the effort to change them, we cannot develop into man number four. If we have two sides developed very well but one that we do not want to work on, this will also hold up our development from becoming a "balanced man," man number four.

One feature of the Fourth Way is that instead of just working on one aspect of ourselves, we work simultaneously on the physical body, the emotions, and the intellect. When working on the physical body, for example, we can also be working on our emotions and intellect. The Fourth Way requires the development of all our centers.

If we omit any of our centers—for example, ignoring our bodies, it will hold us up from becoming balanced. Since each of us is unique, with different strengths and weaknesses, the Fourth Way can tailor a program for us so we do what is needed to develop. For example, a person who is very intellectual, but has a weak and uncoordinated body, does not need more intellectual work but, perhaps, needs workouts in a gym or some other form of physical activity. Hiking, yoga, Pilates, or bicycling can improve one's body. Someone who has a strong intellect but is not very handy with his hands might benefit much more from a woodworking class rather than one on French literature. (I only hope that by the time you are reading this book, I myself have enrolled in a woodworking class rather than, as more likely, started another book.) Moreover, when we are working in one area, for example, at the gym to develop our bodies, we can simultaneously work on the other areas by being aware of our mental attitude and our emotions as we pursue the physical activities. This is a process that will take us many years and there are no shortcuts on the road to self-development.

The Work, besides classifying man according to his development by number, also has a diagrammatic view of man.

Man as a Three-Story Structure

In many ancient parables, man is seen as a house. The Work views man diagrammatically as a three-story house having lower, middle and upper stories. A different center is housed in each story. In the upper story resides the Intellectual Center, in the middle story

119

resides the Emotional Center, and in the lower story or basement of the house resides the Instinctive/Sex and Moving Centers.

This structure is not filled with tables, chairs, and other furniture; rather, it is full of man's different inner states. It is the house of our being. It is a psychological world made up of our thoughts and feelings. Among the possessions in our house are our attitudes, habits, and prejudices, which usually correspond to the lower rooms in us. Unless we develop ourselves, we live in the basement of our house where we live in a state of negative emotions, identification, and internal considering. Therefore, while we can live physically in a very beautiful house with fine furniture, if our inner state (where we really live) is ugly, we live in the shabby basement or lowest story of our psychological house.

We do not enjoy the physical house except to impress others. When impressing others our False Personality governs us. Occasionally, we hear some idea or feel some emotion that lifts us to higher levels of our psychological house but, usually, we fall back into the basement or lower story where we regularly live a life of complaining, awash in a sea of negative emotions. We live there because we are asleep and not aware that we could live in much higher levels with much healthier inner states.

We enter a physical house through the door, and the question is what and how mental impressions enter our psychological house and what their effect is on us.

Food, Air and Impressions

We have organs that take ingredients into our bodies that are necessary for life, i.e., the mouth—food; the nose and mouth—air; and the eyes and ears—impressions. The Work considers impressions the most important food we take in.

We know that food is essential for health. We are progressing through an entire evolution as to our thoughts on food. We know that some plants are not suitable food for man, such as certain mushrooms. As one mushroom expert so aptly put it: "All mushrooms are edible, but some only once." We have learned that not having key nutrients can cause many diseases. Inadequate Vitamin C causes scurvy; lack of certain B vitamins causes beriberi; inadequate vitamin D causes rickets and poor bone structure. We subsequently have also learned that certain foods, such as saturated fat found in meat and dairy products, increase our chances of getting heart disease and certain types of cancer. We know, but many people choose to ignore, that overeating causes obesity and the many health problems that go along with it, e.g., high blood pressure and diabetes.

The process of digestion is to take food into our mouth and break it down into finer and finer particles so that the body can absorb it. The food we put in our mouth is chewed and broken down into a mush called pumas. This is swallowed into our stomach and is broken up by acids and digestive enzymes to form tiny particles such as amino acids from protein, fatty acids from fat, and simple sugars from carbohydrates. These substances are much smaller and lighter than what we took into our mouth. Our bodies absorb them, and what cannot be absorbed, such as fiber, is excreted from our body through our colon. The Work says this is an intricate process of six steps, and anywhere along the line a breakdown (the wrong work) can interfere with the process. We all know that being angry and upset while eating, for example, can interfere with proper digestion. Eating too much can cause interference with the processes of digestion. Exercise will benefit digestion, and lack of exercise will hinder it.

The next thing we take into our bodies through our nose and mouth is air. Air is much more important than food since we can go long periods of time without food, but if we do not get air into our bodies for even a few minutes, we will suffer irreversible damage or death. Our brains are particularly sensitive to a lack of air and its life-giving oxygen. Even a very brief period without air can cause permanent damage to the brain. Air goes through various changes from the time it enters our body until it is exhaled. Our lungs have many cilia to catch unhealthy particles. The air is warmed as it passes through our body. The most important change is that in our lungs the air gives up its oxygen and takes on carbon dioxide, which subsequently leaves the body when we exhale.

What the Work emphasizes is that in addition to food and air, we also take impressions into our body. These impressions or images that enter our eyes are vital to our survival. Impressions can also come in through our senses of hearing and touch. They are happening continuously. To deprive one of incoming impressions will cause severe consequences to the human psychological state, and can even cause death.

Impressions are all external events that occur in our lives that we can react to in one way or another, such as coming into contact with another person, stubbing our toe, or winning the lottery. We know that infants may receive the proper food, but if they are not touched, cuddled, and paid attention to, they curl up and go into a diseased state called Hospitalism. Death can result from this disease. The consequences of not receiving impressions, the food for the mind, are debilitating throughout life. Fortunately, the vast majority of babies are bombarded with external impressions, and that is how we develop, as much as from the food we eat. These incoming impressions continue for the rest of our lives.

As adults who are receiving incoming impressions, we are faced with a totally different problem. Impressions are all events or people that come through our senses and fall on certain areas of our psychic machinery. Because they fall on the same area all the time, we react in the same mechanical way to these incoming impressions. It has been observed that the difference between being in a rut and being in the grave is the depth. If we always act in the same way, our life will always remain the way it has been. The Work says that our level of being attracts our life, and it is our level of being that determines where the impressions fall in our psychic machinery.

If these incoming impressions do not go through a transformation when entering our bodies, they fall on certain parts of our centers, the mechanical parts. The mechanical parts respond mechanically. If, for example, we can't find something, the mechanical reaction will be to become upset through our particular form of negative emotion, whether becoming angry, cursing, or a temper tantrum. Therefore, unless we have a conscious shock, the incoming impression will land on these mechanical centers. For food, we have the digestive system to transform the food into nutrients that are useful for our body. For air, we have the lungs to absorb oxygen and exhale carbon dioxide, but we have no machinery to transform our impressions. We must do it ourselves by our own conscious effort, and that is why the Work is sometimes called Psycho-Transformation.

The form of this conscious shock is a battle between "yes" and "no." The "yes" response is to just follow our automatic mechanical reaction to the incoming impression. This places us in a negative state. We could say "no" psychologically to this automatic response and not go into a negative state.

To say "no", we need the first conscious shock, which is called self-remembering. A simple example might be when we are about to leave our home, we go to where we usually have our keys and they are not there. If our usual reaction is to blow up, that is the mechanical reaction to the impression of our keys not being where they are supposed to be. We lose force by this mechanical reaction because it is negative, and it can literally ruin our whole day because of the energy wasted in furiously looking for our keys and using all sorts of curse words as we search for them.

When we see that our keys are not there, we have a window of opportunity to change the impression that comes into us. We have to do it at the very moment we see the keys are not there, or the window of opportunity is lost. I can hear the reader thinking, "How can we change the sensory data that comes into us?" What we see is that the keys are not there—we can't change that. The Work says that by the process of Divided Attention we can simultaneously see that the keys are not there and also change our mental reaction to the keys not being there and, therefore, we can change the impression coming into us. Granted, it is not absolutely simultaneous, but it is very close to it.

Divided Attention

The Work defines self-remembering technically as two arrows pointing in opposite directions. We are looking out at the external world but we are also looking in at our thoughts about what we are seeing in the external world. Usually, we are just looking out. When we can do both at the same time and see our internal observations as we look at an external object, this is called Divided Attention.

The Work says that this is much more difficult to do than one might think. Try looking at an external object for a minute and observing your internal reactions about it. Although it is difficult, part of the Work is learning to use Divided Attention. If we can learn to use it, we can change the impressions coming into us. For example, at the moment we see that our keys are missing. We can say "no" to just acting mechanically and think to ourselves, "This has happened before. I always do find them. It's no big deal. I have an extra set of keys so I'll take them and my usual keys after." Instead of reacting mechanically, we can observe that we have misplaced our keys again.

The key (no pun intended), is to change awareness, not

violently reacting or identifying. We can change the impression coming into us. If we don't do it the instant we see the keys are missing, we go down the negative path, identifying with our misplaced keys and becoming totally upset, and our actions may upset others around us. At the moment we see the keys missing, we can transform the impression coming into us and prevent the negative state from establishing itself in us.

While the misplacing of our keys seems a very mundane example, the principle applies to all areas of our life, whether we have just learned that we have a serious illness or a financial setback. The Work says that it takes a long time to start remembering ourselves and changing the impressions as they come into us, and that at first we must work on the small things like not blowing up when we misplace our keys. Remembering ourselves is a much more serious matter, taking years of practice. By doing this we also raise our level of being.

Beginners in the Work must make realistic goals that they can accomplish. Not getting negative over the misplaced keys would be an example of a place we could start. Other examples might be: not blowing up at waiters, store clerks or being placed on hold when we make a phone call, not becoming upset at having to listen to a voice menu and push numbers when we call an organization or having to wash the dishes, take out the trash or a million other details of daily living.

It should be pointed out that even in such simple matters as misplacing our keys, it is not always possible to remember ourselves and transform the impressions as they enter us. If we could do that all the time we would be fully conscious beings, which we are not.

The Work says that it is still possible to transform impressions after the event and, therefore, change our view of them. We all remember things we may have thought were bad while they were happening to us, but later reflecting on the event and changed our minds and thought what we experienced was good for us. The Work says that whereas we have stomachs to transform food, we have the Work to transform the impressions that come to us.

The Work is our mental stomach. It is best to transform the impressions as they enter us. We can use the Work and think in a new way, thereby transforming the impressions. The Work suggests that, at the end of the day, or the next day, or even years later, we review the events that transpired and see if we can't transform the ones that we thought were negative while they were happening and change them into a positive or at least neutral mode. In this way, the Work says we have the power not only to change our present, but the past as well.

By being able to transform impressions, we can leave the basement of our psychological space where most of us live and go to higher places, such as entering the living room where life becomes psychologically more comfortable for us because we now have the ability to identify less with events and are less likely to fall into negative emotions, and remember ourselves more. In order to transform impressions we must observe our internal state as well as our external state by the Work method of Divided Attention. And in order to develop the ability to practice Divided Attention, we need to understand the levels of attention.

The Three Levels of Attention

The Work says there are three levels of attention. The first is zero-attention, which characterizes mechanical divisions of centers. An example of zero-attention is when we read a page of a book and don't remember a thing, or wash the dishes while thinking of other things. The second form of attention does not require effort, but is simply attracted to the external event. Examples of this might be looking at an attractive member of the opposite sex or walking down a street and witnessing an auto accident. The third type of attention must be directed by effort and will. This is the attention required in dividing attention and is the foundation of self-remembering. By placing our conscious attention internally, as well as on the external event as it is happening, it is possible to change our internal reactions to it.

Let's go back to the misplaced keys. We separate ourselves from the event that has taken place. We are not that event. According to the Work, life can and should be seen as a series of events, not merely as people, places, and things. A person or thing does not become an event until we make some contact with it. If we can observe internally that we are caught up in a particular event, the act of internal attention makes it possible not to identify with the event so much. The misplaced keys may seem like an easy example, but it still takes practice not to become identified with it. To do so is to keep our cool when we see that the keys are not where they should be.

Moreover, since only a certain number of events in our lives constantly recur, we can apply divided attention when we see them arise. We can label them. Some examples might be: "This is called worrying about an illness"; "This is called being blamed for something I did not do"; "This is called being overlooked"; "This is called being disappointed"; "This is called being in a mess"; "This is called being in a state of indecision"; "This is called being late"; and so on. If we can label it, we will not identify so much with it. In order to label it, however, we must make the effort to pay attention to what is going on internally while an event is happening externally. We must also be able to observe what inner state we are in.

Inner States vs. External Events

We talked briefly above about events. An event can be anything we come directly in contact with. A book lying on a table is not an event, but once we pick up the book and start reading it, the book becomes an event in our lives. So events are anything, whether it is people or objects, with which we come into contact. Each of our lives is a series of events. We have the ability to expand events or contract events. Usually events that displease us are those we expand. If we think someone insulted us, we can carry that event all day, and in fact, for the rest of our lives. Most people are familiar with someone who went through a lawsuit or medical operation that did not turn out well, and the person carries that event with him for the rest of his life and the event becoming that person's major source of conversation. Usually events that please us are not carried with us as long, but we can also expand these events. A kind word or compliment can stay with us for years. We do have the ability to choose which external events we want to place our emphasis on. Whether we see the glass half full or half empty is within our power.

Inner states are what we are feeling internally. The difference between an external event and an inner state is that inner states usually last a lot longer than a single external event. Moreover, we usually think we are the inner state rather than just observing it. Let's say we are depressed. This depression can last hours, months, or sometimes years. When we are depressed we think this state is us. We never try to separate this state from our real self by observing, for example, that "Friedman is depressed" and not doing so colors our whole interior life, which in reality is our life. There are, of course, other states that we take ourselves to be. Some people live in a very hostile state and are continually angry. They are usually angry with themselves, which then colors all external events. Some people are in a manic state, which eventually turns into a depressed state. Some people are in a sad state, some in a guilty state, and a few in a happy state. The people in these various states think they *are* the state and never make any effort to separate themselves from it.

Let us suppose we have a piece of wood. We then glue another piece of wood to it. The two pieces of wood now look like a single piece. It is possible to separate the piece of wood that was glued to the original piece, but it is not easy. It will take effort. The two pieces of wood will, under ordinary circumstances, never separate by themselves. It is the same thing with our inner states. Separating ourselves from our inner states takes considerable effort. The Work tells us that these inner states, which we take as ourselves, can ruin our lives and lead to all sorts of violence and unhappiness. They are part of our inner psychological life. Just as we are responsible for how we drive our cars on the highway, we are responsible for how we drive our inner psychological states in our inner life. If we are negative for more than a very short period of time, all sorts of disasters will enter our lives that would not have entered if we were in a positive state. The question arises as to how we can separate ourselves from these states that we feel are us.

The answer the Work gives always comes back to self-remembering. If we do not identify with the state but say, "There goes Friedman again in one of his depressed states," or "There goes Friedman again in his angry state," we have made a huge start. It doesn't mean the negative state will go away immediately, although it could. Even if the negative state doesn't go away, at least we were able to recognize it and therefore get the slightest degree of separation between the state and ourselves. It might seem like a very minor step to just realize that we are in a depressed state even if we can't get out of it, but the person who doesn't realize he is in a state of depression will probably not seek help because he thinks the depressed state is him, and there is nothing to separate from. The mere fact, however, of recognition is like taking the first step in prying up the corner of the two glued pieces of wood and realizing they are really two pieces and not just one. To realize they are two pieces is a very big step toward eventually being able to separate them. If we thought they were just one piece, we would never even make an attempt to separate them.

As was mentioned in the Work's Law of the Pendulum, all

things, including inner states, swing from one extreme to the other. If we realize this, then when we are in one state, we can know that eventually it will swing into the opposite state. As the saying goes in Vipassana, one of the two main types of Buddhist meditation, "This too will pass." The goal of the Work, of course, is to catch the pendulum in the middle balance point so we don't swing from being depressed to being manic, but achieve a balanced state in the center.

What self-remembering does is to allow us to draw the feeling of 'I' out of these inner states. We are not depressed: "Friedman is depressed," or "Johnson is depressed," and we are not Friedman or Johnson. By self-observation of the state we are in, we no longer identify completely with the inner state and its negative train of thought in ourselves. Identification is putting the feeling of 'I' into whatever happens. We get a cold; we identify with it and are miserable. We are in a depressed state and because we identify with it and put our feeling of 'I' into it, we are very unhappy and might do violence to others or especially to ourselves. The key is not to take the negative state as ourselves, but to say "Friedman is angry" rather than saying, "I am angry" which avoids placing our sense of self in this negativity. This is crucial because the one thing the Work asks us to sacrifice in ourselves is our suffering.

Sacrificing Our Suffering

One of the purposes of the Work is to effect a change of being. If we stay the same, then we can't change our being. To change our being we must sacrifice something. All esoteric schools of transformation ask us to sacrifice something. Even modern religions encourage their congregations to sacrifice a portion of their earnings, often ten percent, to the church as a tithing. Supposedly for every dollar tithed, ten times that amount will come back to us. The Work doesn't ask for any financial sacrifices, although I feel sure many of the followers of Gurdjieff and Ouspensky did give financial support. The Work asks us to give up something considerably greater than money or any other possessions. The Work asks us to give up just one thing: our suffering.

This is not as easy as one would think. In fact, it is extremely difficult. Everyone has his or her own particular form of suffering. As Tolstoy once observed about marriage, "All happy marriages are happy in the same way and all unhappy marriages are unhappy in different ways." So, as to suffering, we all have our own specialty. Some groups seem to specialize in it. Milton Berle, the famous comedian, and Jewish himself, observed that the reason Jews don't drink is because it interferes with their suffering. We all suffer in some way. Our job according to the Work is to observe ourselves to determine what our own particular form of suffering is. We cannot rise to a higher level of being unless we give up our present form of suffering.

We can suffer from just about anything. Let us start with the suffering between man and woman. A man can suffer because he has never found a woman who understands him or because he is not appreciated for being the provider. A woman can suffer from not being able to find a partner, or if she has, he is insensitive or a slob. The couple can suffer from not being able to have children or from having too many. Then there is the area of suffering concerning parents and children. Our parents never understood us. They didn't treat us as well as they did one of our siblings. Our children don't respect us and teenagers seem to be ashamed of us. Clarence Darrow, the great lawyer, adroitly summed up this form of suffering by his remark, "The first half of life is ruined by our parents and the second half by our children."

There are certain general areas of suffering. There is the whole area of "if only." If only I had finished my education; if only I didn't have this disease; if only we had not gone on that vacation; if only we had gone on that vacation; if only the war had ended a few months earlier; if only I had more money; if only I had sold my stocks a few months earlier; if only my spouse didn't drink so much; if only I had a better tennis serve, and so on. All of these "if only's" are connected with our suffering and must be sacrificed. Another form of suffering is the sense of failure. This is a more subtle form of suffering that some people even enjoy. It is the idea that, "I tried to make the marriage, business, or whatever work, but I failed." It's as if we think that we made all the effort possible and somehow it just didn't work out. We glory in our own suffering.

Whatever the particular form of suffering we have, according to the Work, all sufferings have certain characteristics. Each suffering carries a self-justification. We justify our suffering, and it becomes part of us. We become chained to our suffering. We complain about it but cling to it. Our suffering becomes the baggage that we are always dragging behind us or pushing in front of us.

Sometimes this is very easy to see in others. As discussed earlier, we can expand an external event so it becomes almost our whole life; the person, for example, who had an operation that did not come out as hoped and then he spends years or even the rest of his life reliving it, and in general lets this particular suffering dominate his life. He complains about it to everyone until everyone who can, avoids him. Another obvious example might be someone who goes through a legal problem, such as a divorce, and feels he received "the short end of the stick." He never gets over the divorce or lawsuit and considers writing a book about the injustice he has suffered. Fortunately, for the rest of us, few of these books ever get written.

These people let the so-called injustice dominate their lives long after the event. Sometimes they let it dominate the rest of their lives. We sometimes see whole groups or nations with a collective suffering about some event, such as a battle that they continually suffer from and always talk about. Then when we ask when the battle took place, which by the intensity of their suffering we think was a few months or years ago or at least in their lifetime, we learn the battle over the "Bridge at Ollie" took place six hundred years ago.

By justifying our suffering we make it legitimate. What other choice do we have in our circumstances but to suffer? Suffering always comes from our own idea of justice: what happened to us isn't fair. Everyone, therefore, justifies his or her suffering. Because life has not gone the way we expected or hoped it would go, life is just not fair and we cling to our own sense of justice. The Work points out that we cannot justify ourselves on our own sense of justice, and we start to realize this as we apply the Work ideas to ourselves.

The particular form of suffering we endure drags us down. We lose force by it. All our internal considering and account making when people have treated us unfairly or owe us something stem from our suffering. All our suffering is acquired in life, and since each person's personality is different, we all have our own forms of suffering. The Work says we cannot work on ourselves and therefore change our being unless we give up our suffering. The Work says that giving up our suffering is possible, just very difficult.

The question arises as to why it is so difficult to give up our suffering. On the surface we would think everyone would be glad to give up the suffering that makes us so unhappy. The answer the Work gives goes back to the concept that we are not one unified person either over time or at a particular moment. We have many different 'I's, each with its own personality. Unfortunately, we have a group of 'I's in us who really enjoy suffering and making us unhappy. These 'I's do not want to go away. They want to preserve themselves and even dominate us, just as other 'I's in us do. Unless we can become aware of these negative 'I's in us by observing them through the process of self-observation, which is the key method of the Work, these 'I's will continue to dominate us and keep us suffering and unhappy.

A Shortcut to Relieving Our Suffering:
Liking What We Dislike

The Work offers a shortcut for relieving our suffering. It is a simple solution, but being simple doesn't mean it is easy. If we can learn to like what we dislike, we will suffer much less. We want certain things that we don't have, and we would like to get rid of some things we do have. In both situations we dislike what we don't have or certain things we do have, and we suffer from each of these conditions.

It is, of course, not easy to like what we dislike, especially concerning the people we relate to in our lives, so the Work offers some intermediate steps to help us in this direction. The first intermediate step is deciding not to object to something we dislike. Nicoll gives an example from when he was a student of Gurdjieff at his institute in France. Nicoll was given the job of shoveling out the manure from the barn, hardly an enjoyable task, and certainly not an easy one to like. Nicoll came up with a solution: although he could not find it within his power to like shoveling out the manure, he decided that he would not object to it. It was something that had to be done. This made the task easier for Nicoll.

While reading Nicoll's description of this situation, the following situation occurred in my life. I had a minor operation, and a complication set in. I had to change my bandages several times a day because of drainage. I certainly disliked doing this but, on reading Nicoll's experience, I decided that I would not object to it. It was what I had to do. The changing of bandages went on for several weeks. Although I never got to like changing them, not objecting to the task made the changing of the bandages much easier. I became much more proficient at it and, in the end, I actually stopped disliking it. I just took it as something that had to be done. After several weeks the drainage stopped, and my task of changing the bandages was over.

This brings up the second step in the shortcut to relieving our suffering, which is that we can stop disliking what we dislike and become neutral toward it. Nowhere is this more important than in our relationship with the people in our lives. The Work says that one of the ways we know we are progressing in the Work is that we are willing to accept the unpleasant manifestations of other people. If we can go from disliking these manifestations to being neutral about them, we will have made a big advance in doing the Work and in raising our consciousness and relieving our suffering.

We all know we have unpleasant manifestations in ourselves that could upset others. The Work says that what we see that is unpleasant in others we also have to some extent in ourselves. Therefore, by learning to accept the unpleasant manifestations in others, we are also learning to accept our own unpleasant aspect, and once we see the same quality in ourselves we will get a different picture of what we are really like. This will result in raising our consciousness.

On an even more personal level, if we could learn to like what we dislike about ourselves, we would greatly reduce our suffering. One area that is very important in this regard is our diseases and physical disabilities. On the surface it seems it would be very hard to learn to like our diseases and disabilities. For most of us, including myself, we become so identified with our illnesses and disabilities that we become them. Our whole life is wrapped up in them. According to the Work, these illnesses and disabilities are exactly the material we need in life to work on, to fight becoming identified with and to not put our sense of 'I' in them. This is extremely difficult for most of us, and certainly not easy for beginners in the Work. However, it has been done. Susan Jeffers, for example, in her book, *Feel the Fear and Do It Anyway*, discusses this under the concept of "Saying yes to your universe."

If we blame circumstances and others for what happens to us, we always remain victims, and in the Work terminology we are always in negative states with all the harmful consequences these negative states bring. According to the Work, most of our illnesses are psychologically caused by our negative states and the stress we place ourselves under. In her book, Jeffers also describes people who feel glad because of their illness since it changed their lives in many beneficial ways.

I know of one woman who was under several severe stresses. Her husband was dying of cancer, she was making numerous daily juice drinks to help his condition, and they were the owners of a retail shop. Since her husband was unable to attend to the business, she felt she had to do everything connected with it. She also had to take care of her child who was still living at home. She developed breast cancer shortly after her husband passed away. She stopped going to the store and delegated others to run it; she stopped worrying about her daughter and she started dancing on a more regular basis. In fact, she danced her way through chemotherapy and is still dancing.

Another woman I know survived cervical cancer and decided

that her life was going by, and she wasn't doing the things she wanted and enjoyed doing, which in her case was traveling. She and her husband started taking trips and cruises that she had always wanted to take but hadn't been able to fit into her busy schedule. Now she makes such trips her first priority. Both of these women say they never would have changed their lifestyles for the better if it hadn't been for the cancer they experienced. It may not happen in many cases, but it does happen. It is possible to like what we dislike, to reconstruct our experiences and events and see them in a positive light. If we can like what we dislike, or in the phrase Susan Jeffers uses, "say yes to your universe," we can go a long way toward eliminating our mechanical suffering. The Work makes a distinction between mechanical and conscious suffering.

The Difference Between Mechanical
and Conscious Suffering

By mechanical suffering, the Work means that the suffering is automatic and instantaneous. We come down with an illness, and we automatically start suffering. The same is true if we lose our money, our relationship, or even misplace our keys. The way we have learned to take in impressions from the outside world and act in mechanical ways to these outside events becomes our life. The way to change our lives is not to change our external circumstances, but to change the way we react to them. If we always act the same way, we will always remain the same and our being can never change.

In fact, our level of being is how we react to the events in our lives. It is not something mysterious. If external events continually upset us, we have a low level of being. The person who is angry at almost everything that happens has a very low level of being. The person who takes things calmly, who allows things to roll over him rather than being upset, has a much higher level of being. When bad things happen to him, he says to himself, "This too shall pass," because he knows that things are continually changing, going from one side of the pendulum to the other, even if he isn't consciously aware of this particular law. He cannot be thrown off base by external events. Most of us fall between these two extremes, and so our level of being is also between these two levels.

Of course, the question arises as to why we always react in the same mechanical ways to external events. The answer is that these ways are ingrained in us. They have formed deep grooves as on a record and once these grooves have been established they are extremely difficult to change. Another way of viewing the difficulty of changing our mechanical reactions to external events is that our emotions are so much quicker than our intellectual thoughts. We can tell ourselves intellectually that we will not get upset the next time we misplace our keys, but when the keys are not there and we are late for an appointment, our emotions instantly blow up. Or take the more serious case of breaking up with our partner. We drive by our ex's home and see her new romantic interest's car parked outside. We go crazy! The emotions are triggered so fast that the intellect and Intellectual Center are left in the dust.

In the novel *Man's Fate* by the French novelist André Malraux, a Chinese man is married to a French nurse, and they are living in China. They have agreed to have an open relationship where each can relate sexually with others. The nurse tells her husband that she has had a sexual encounter with a physician, and her husband goes mad with rage. The saying, "Logic is good for the mind but not for the gut," applies here. In all these situations, our response is instantaneous and automatic. In a split second we identify with the situation and go into a negative state, and justify it by the particular circumstance it occurred in.

Mechanical suffering is the common lot of mankind. When we acquired our personality, which is essential for our growth in life, we also acquired certain ways of reacting to the external events of life, the impressions we are constantly taking in. Because we always react in the same mechanical way, we always remain the same. What applies to individuals also applies to couples and nations. In many relationships, once one person makes a remark and the other responds in an automatic way, the whole conversation could take place without the people in the room and just a recording playing, with each making mechanical comments to each other. All this mechanical suffering is what the Work asks us to sacrifice. It wants us to think in new ways so we can act in new ways rather than in old mechanical ways.

Although the Work wants us to sacrifice our mechanical suffering, which always makes us lose force, it encourages conscious suffering, which always increases our force. Conscious suffering is never automatic and instantaneous. It always requires a conscious effort. Conscious suffering connects us with our Higher Centers, while mechanical suffering makes our Higher Centers unavailable to us; we can't connect with them because of all the static in our lives. Conscious suffering always creates more force, while mechanical suffering always drains our force. Conscious suffering opens our being up to higher levels, whereas mechanical suffering drives our being down to lower levels. Perhaps the best way to obtain a glimpse of this is to give some examples.

A mother comes home from her job, and after finishing housework and making dinner, is exhausted. Her young daughter asks her to read to her before she goes to bed. The mother agrees to read to her. When she finishes, she sees how happy her daughter is, and she has more energy and feels better about herself.

Gina comes home from work tired. She has signed up for a yoga class, but doesn't feel like going. She'd rather just take it easy and watch TV than put in the effort to go to class. She decides that she made the commitment to herself to go to that class and decides to go. After the class she feels so much better, not only from the class, but because she kept the commitment to herself.

Jim has decided he wants to write a novel. He has a job he must commute to and a family to support. The only time he could do any writing and have the privacy to do it is if he gets up earlier each morning. He decides to get up each morning at 5:45 a.m. and write for an hour before he starts his regular day. He keeps to his schedule despite other obligations he has, even when he is very tired from a hard day before. After a year he completes his novel. Jim feels great and has much more energy in his life than before he started to get up early. He feels much better about himself and even if he can't get the novel published, he has accomplished one of his long-time dreams by writing it. He is getting along better with his family and his colleagues at work and is looking forward to starting a second novel.

George, a soldier, risks his own life while in battle to try to save the life of one of his buddies. No one saw what George did, and he is not looking for any recognition for his actions. Maybe that is why veterans of wars always relive their battle experiences. That was a period when the soldiers experienced conscious suffering and not the mechanical suffering they experience back home. People often act with much conscious suffering during wars or civil emergencies, when they make conscious sacrifices to help others without any motive of personal gain, and often risk their lives.

One of the great examples of conscious suffering was Rosa Parks, the African-American woman who in December 1955 in Montgomery, Alabama refused to move to the back of the bus because of the color of her skin. She was arrested for her action, but it led to the boycott of the buses by African-Americans and was a key incident in the civil rights movement.

In all the examples given of conscious suffering, we have people who were aware of the suffering they were experiencing. It was not mechanical. However, the Work teaches an antidote to going into a negative state.

We Have a Right Not to be Negative

According to the Work, if nothing could ever turn us into a negative state, we would be fully conscious beings. The Work teaches, however, that it is extremely easy to fall into a negative state. Gurdjieff said that negative emotions are what the world runs on. From the Work's perspective, it is very easy to fall into a negative state and then justify it under the particular set of circumstances that allowed us to become negative. The Work says, *we have a right not to be negative.* Notice that the Work doesn't say, "We have no right to be negative." Rather, it gives us the right not to be negative. This is a very valuable right that few people use.

When things do not go according to our expectations we naturally want to blame others, or circumstances. Victor E. Frankl explored the fact that we can choose our thoughts, no matter what the external circumstances. He described his experiences as an inmate in a concentration camp in his book, *Man's Search for Meaning.* He remembered men comforting others and giving away their last piece of bread. He says that although there were not many who did this, those who did offered sufficient proof that everything can be taken away from a man but one thing. This Frankl refers to as the last of our human freedoms—the right to choose one's attitude in any situation, to choose one's own way.

The Work says we are always to blame if we are negative— never other people or external circumstances. We are responsible for

145

our own inner state. On the other hand, the Work holds as equally ridiculous the idea that we will stop going into negative states once we know we are responsible for them. It takes many years of doing the Work before we can even approach the level of staying permanently out of negative states. What the Work asks is that we keep trying to not go into them and separate ourselves once we realize we are in them. It takes lots of falling into and getting out of negative states and there are no shortcuts.

The Work emphasizes the right we have not to be negative as one of our most important rights and it should be cultivated. "I have a right not to be negative" might be one of the few mantras of the Work. I typed it up and placed the message in different places in my house to remind myself. Not that it works every time or when major things happen, but even the smallest event that does not go as we planned can quickly turn us into a negative state. This reminder has helped me in small matters from becoming negative.

Not becoming negative is also a form of self-remembering, of feeling a trace of our Real 'I'. This lifts us above the level of our negative 'I's that are all telling us, instantaneously and mechanically, that we have a right to be negative, especially in the particular circumstances we are facing. Instead of looking at the person or event that has made us negative, it is also helpful to look within ourselves to see which negative 'I' we are currently hearing. For example, as I am writing this I have a bad cold and my voice is very hoarse. There is a negative 'I' in me saying, "Poor Friedman, I have a right to feel miserable." It's my 'I' of self-pity. If I keep on listening to it, I will

146

become more miserable and lose more force, but I don't have to buy into this negative 'I'. I have the right not to be negative and instead work on this book and do what I can today, cold and sore throat or not.

Every negative 'I's only purpose is to take hold of us and feed upon us and strengthen itself at our expense. According to the Work, the cause of negative states is negative 'I's that live only to persuade us with their half-truths and lies (my cold will ruin my day) and therefore rule over us and spoil our lives. To observe these negative 'I's is not easy. On the other hand, it is worth the effort because negative states are what Hell is all about. As John Milton said in *Paradise Lost*, "The Mind is its own place and can make a Heaven of Hell or a Hell of Heaven." When we are in a negative state we are in Hell regardless of our external environment.

By taking the responsibility for being in a negative state rather than blaming someone else for putting us there, we are reversing how we usually think. We are thinking in a new way. One of the purposes of the Work is to make us think in new ways, to break our habitual ways of thinking. This is the beginning of our transformation and that is what the Work is about.

The Work suggests that we can ask ourselves when we are on the threshold of becoming negative, "What will it matter a hundred years from today?" Since almost nothing we do will matter in a hundred years, or perhaps in a few weeks, or by the end of the day, or even possibly in a few minutes, this is a reminder against becoming negative. Becoming negative is always a choice we make. Another suggestion the Work makes is that we observe our moods. If we do,

147

they will be less likely to take such big swings and put us in such deep negative states. All these suggestions as to how we can avoid entering a negative state when events do not go as hoped or expected are really based on our ability to remember ourselves.

Remembering ourselves is the first conscious shock and depends on our observing ourselves and separating from ourselves by saying, for example, "There goes Friedman worrying again about another matter that will turn out all right." If we make no separation between the Real 'I' and what Friedman is doing, it is not possible to remember ourselves, and if we take what Friedman is doing as his Real 'I', separation is impossible, and we cannot observe ourselves.

The Work says there are three indications that we are doing the Work. One is that we are better able to keep to our aims. If we say we will do something, we do it. If we promise to call someone at a certain time, we call him at that time. The Work says this indicates that our various I's are becoming more unified, and we are developing a Deputy Steward to help keep us on the course we set.

Another indication that we are doing the Work is that we are more tolerant of the unpleasant manifestations of others that used to annoy us so. It is the realization that what we see in others is really in ourselves as well, so we become more tolerant of others, as well as ourselves. In fact, according to the Work, even more important, than bearing the unpleasant manifestations of others, is to bear the unpleasant manifestations of ourselves. If we justify everything we do, we are preventing ourselves from working on ourselves.

All esoteric teachings emphasize patience because the more we

148

can patiently endure things, whether it is the unpleasant manifestations of others or ourselves is a sign of the development of our being. Those people who "fly off the handle" at the slightest provocation whether it is to their children, partners, strangers, or those less fortunate than ourselves, have a lower level of being than those who can patiently wait out a situation. The less we can stand, the lower our level of being. If we notice where we lose our temper or become negative, this indicates we have come to the edge of our level of being.

The Importance of Relaxation and Exercise

Gurdjieff said that there are only two things we should do every day. One is to remember ourselves, and the other is to relax. "Ordinary man", Gurdjieff observed—"even if he comes to the conclusion that work on himself is indispensable—is the slave of his body…. One of the first things a man must learn is to observe and feel muscular tension and to be able to relax the unnecessary tension of the muscles when it is necessary." The Work says that we are continually building up tension in our muscles, and this tension is responsible for many of our illnesses. Specifically, the Work says we should try to relax the small muscles in our face, particularly those around our nose, eyes, and under our chin. The tiny muscles in our toes and hands are also very important. One suggestion, if we have only a little time, is to let our hands hang over a chair and relax the muscles in our wrists. We have to concentrate and see if we can really feel these muscles and release them. In a sense it is like Vipassana, a form of Buddhist meditation in which the meditator looks within to witness how everything is changing within him all the time. If we can concentrate on these small muscles and relax them, we can then go to the larger muscles in our body. Even things such as our posture are dependent on these tiny muscles. For example we can stand up tall, but if the muscles in our face are tight they will show our strained emotional state regardless of how straight our larger muscles are holding us up.

Furthermore, the Work says that if we are in the Moving Center and continually rushing about, this will have an effect on our Emotional Center, and we will feel all our emotions are rushed. Therefore, practicing relaxation daily is a way to not only release tension but change the center we are functioning under. Of course, this takes a tremendous amount of effort but, according to Maurice Nicoll, if we concentrate on relaxing these small muscles once a week, we will obtain significant results. Although concentrating on small muscles is very important in the Work, it should not detract from the importance of overall movement.

What follows is my own extrapolation of the Work, not something I have read directly in it. I know that Gurdjieff used to have his students do dance movements, and although I do not know what these dance movements were except possibly whirling, I would say that dance in any form is very good for us. The fact of the matter is that rigor mortis does not set in just when a person dies. It seems to me it starts about age twenty-five, and we continue to become more rigid as we get older. One just has to see an old person walking down the street with his stiff body, often accompanied by a walking support apparatus, to know what the body looks like in old age. Therefore, any type of movement that fights the growing rigidity of the body is good.

The reason to do these movements is not so much to become more flexible, but to keep us where we are instead of continuing down the road to rigidity. Dance is a great place to start. Whatever form the dancing takes, it offers great benefits. Sufi dancing has the added benefit of combining singing and dancing, and singing is very good for us (opera singers usually live long lives because of their well-developed lungs). Sufi dancing events are held in most large cities under The Dances of Universal Peace. But all sorts of dancing is beneficial, from square dancing to Contra dancing (a type of folk dancing in lines rather than squares), from swing to Latin, to rock and roll. All forms of dancing help keep the body flexible.

Another form of exercise, the king of exercise, is walking. Nothing beats walking for keeping the body in shape with the least chance of injuring oneself. It requires no special equipment and can start from anywhere. No special environment is necessary for taking a walk, and every time of day has its own unique ambiance. I would like to distinguish between taking a walk and walking to do errands or to get someplace where there is a time pressure to get there. In my opinion, this time pressure walking (although much better than no walking) does not have the psychological benefits of a "useless" walk, where there is no specific destination and no deadline to return. It is also my opinion that all this talk about walking at a brisk pace to bring the heart rate up, although possibly good for the heart, creates another type of pressure that defeats the psychological benefits of walking. A walk at any pace for any time over ten or fifteen minutes has a very soothing and at the same time energizing effect on the body. It is soul food for the body.

As to flexibility, there are many disciplines that help keep rigidity at bay. Two that are popular are Tai Chi, which is practiced by millions in China and elsewhere, and yoga. After many years the rigidity has so set in older people that they are not even able to sit on the floor, let alone do any yoga postures. As a person who has been stiff all his life, I feel doing yoga has helped prevent me from getting stiffer, and there are some places where I have actually become slightly more flexible. I now also do Pilates which helps strengthen the entire body, but especially the deep abdominal and core muscles. All forms of exercise help the body to maintain its fluidity. We each should adopt one or more of these and do it on a regular basis no matter how limited our time is. It is as the old Chinese saying goes, "Those who do not find time to exercise will find time for illness." So we must *pay* ourselves first and carry out our exercise program and then do what we have to do. Otherwise, we will find we don't have the time in our busy schedules. The least we should do is take a daily walk. To me this is part of the Work.

Another way to help relax ourselves is to have a pet, especially a cat or dog. The benefit of a dog, besides the constant love he gives you, is in taking him for a walk. Dogs seem to be psychic and know the exact moment you get up with the intention of going on a walk. They get excited and run to the door. Having a dog will encourage you to take more walks, and the petting and playing with them is very good for releasing your tensions. Not walking a dog is an act of cruelty, and

152

those who don't plan to walk their dogs would be better off not having one.

As to cats, as anyone can attest who has one, it is not surprising that the ancient Egyptians worshiped them, and it was supposedly a capital offense to kill a cat. Although a cat may be a "tiger" outside your home and seems to lead a very independent life, when they are in the house they are always babies and you are their mother and they want your affection. In fact, they demand it in many ways. They want to sit or sleep on your lap, and when you stroke them they often go into cat heaven. This is not only good for the cat, but very good in relaxing you. Cats are also psychic and are very aware when you are sick or not feeling right, and they will sit with you for hours and give you incredible emotional support. To have a cat or dog in your home is to have not merely a pet, but also a teacher and a master in the art of relaxation. All pets are useful for helping us to relax and teaching us about all animals, including ourselves. They also are a live entertainment center.

There is another thing we can do for ourselves to help decrease the rate of rigidity taking place in our body, and that is massage. Often we do not even know how tense our muscles are until someone gives us a massage, and we feel the pain and tightness that we were not even aware of before. Hippocrates, the father of medicine, supposedly received a massage every day. Bob Hope, when he went overseas to entertain the troops, supposedly took a masseuse with him to give him massages on the trip. If you can afford it, receive massages regularly. If you can't afford it, get a book about massages and just start exchanging massages with someone who is interested. There are many brief massage classes—from Reflexology to Shiatsu to Swedish massage—given in many adult and alternative education facilities. It is not necessary to take a 120-hour or 500-hour massage course in order to give a massage. The only thing necessary to give a massage is a minimum of knowledge on techniques that many books can give and having the proper intent. I myself have been exchanging massages for many years with different people who have become very good friends in the process.

There is one other activity that I feel is both spiritual and very grounding and that is gardening. There is just something about even the simplest act of digging up weeds that teaches us about our connection with the earth and the universe. There is a glory in picking our own strawberries or other fruits and vegetables from our garden and placing them on our dinner table or into our cooking pots. The beauty of growing flowers brings us closer to the beauty of the universe. To see how plants come from seeds and sprout, blossom, and then die, brings us closer to how there is a time and place for everything in the universe, including us. What can be said about plants outside also applies to houseplants and growing our own sprouts and herbs inside. No matter how small a space we have, growing plants of any type is very uplifting and brings us to a greater degree of awareness. As in other areas of our lives, we sometimes have to fail many times before we finally become competent in this activity.

The only problem with gardening, yoga, or any other activity discussed above is that we can become identified with them. We worry, for example, whether we planted the seeds correctly. Again, we must always try to prevent ourselves from identification with the activities by remembering we are much more than any of these activities.

The Work says we should move our brain every day, meaning we should do some intellectual activity in which we have to think. That is why learning new things, whether they be studying a foreign language, reading a book, attending a play, or going to a concert, are all beneficial.

As to teaching this work to others, the only way we can teach anyone the Way is by our own example. A reporter once asked Dr. Albert Schweitzer if he thought that teaching by example was one way to teach. Schweitzer replied that teaching by example is not one way to teach, but the only way to teach. So unless our own level of being and subsequently our actual behavior rises, we cannot teach anyone else. Just having knowledge of the ideas of the Work without eventually putting them into practice is useless. Perhaps the greatest parable that the Work uses to show what task we face and the difficulties on the way is the parable of the horse-drawn carriage.

The Parable of the Horse-Drawn Carriage

Gurdjieff referred to this parable quite frequently to show the inner state of man and what he must do to change it. Gurdjieff said the driver represents the mind, the carriage the body, and the horse the emotions. The carriage representing the body is in very poor shape; the horse is also in bad shape and in serious need of food; the reins holding the horse are in tatters and can hardly be used. The driver who represents the mind is in really bad shape. He is inside what was then called a "public house," which we now call a bar. The driver is drunk, but the interesting point is what he is drunk on. It is not alcohol but, rather, his imagination. He imagines he has all these qualities such as unity and the ability to do. This is the Imaginary 'I' we discussed earlier. The first problem the driver has is that he must get outside to see the condition of the carriage and horse before he can go anywhere. Instead, the driver sits in the bar full of all sorts of illusions and beliefs of what he can do when actually he can do nothing. Unless he can awaken and leave the bar, the carriage will never go anywhere. So, the first job for the driver is to awaken. Since the driver thinks he is already awake, this can be a very difficult task.

There actually is a play by Eugene O'Neill concerning this point called *The Iceman Cometh*. The entire play takes place in a combination rooming house and bar. All the characters in the play have all these ideas of the things they would like to do, but they just continue sitting in the bar drinking and talking. Then a character arrives in the bar and he starts to plant ideas in these men that they actually can go out and do some of the things they are just talking about. O'Neill, in a very powerful manner, stresses this idea over and over again. Then the character who was stimulating these men to go out and do what they were just talking about committed a crime himself and is arrested and taken away from the bar. The men then go back to just talking about what they hoped to do and never do anything. In terms of the Work, the character in the play who tried to make the men in the bar actually live their dreams in real life rather than just talk about them gave them a shock.

The only way we can stop our illusions of what we can do and actually get out of the bar, is to receive a shock. If we think of the bar as the basement, we mostly live in the basements of our lives and never get to the cleaner air of the outdoors. Another way of viewing the basement, according to the Work, is that the basement represents the mechanical parts of our centers where everything is done mechanically and automatically with no conscious thought involved. This is the main task we all face: we must somehow be given a shock to get out of the basement of our lives and into the open air and to start acting consciously rather than mechanically. This definitely is a step up to a higher level.

Once we go outside, we can actually take a look at the condition of the horse, carriage and reins. The driver also represents the Intellectual Center, the horse represents the Emotional Center, and the reins are the connection between our Emotional and our Intellectual Centers. The tattered reins represent the poor communication between these two centers and why we have so much trouble achieving our aims and goals. We can intellectually decide we want to do something, but if we don't make the emotional connection these aims are never achieved. And since our Emotional Center reacts so much faster than our Intellectual Center, we are controlled by our emotions rather than our intellect.

Only when we strongly feel some aim emotionally as well as intellectually will we reach our goal. According to the Work, the key is that our emotions do not understand any language; they can only visualize. Therefore, if we want to get our emotions involved we must visualize what we want. Visualization is the language of the emotions and therefore the Work says we must visualize our goals, not merely think about them.

There is one other factor that the Work says is important to achieve our goals, and that is that we must attend to our goals by directing our attention to them. If we think of our goals only sporadically, they will fall from the forefront of our mind to the background, and they will simply not have the force to bring about change. We must give constant attention to what we want.

Another aspect of this parable is that even after we feed the horse, repair the carriage and fix the harness and reins, before we can drive the carriage, we must climb up to the box on of the carriage to hold the reins so we can guide the horse. Obviously, we cannot drive the carriage from the ground level. This climbing up to the box represents another level we must go up psychologically before we are able to make the carriage and horse move. Whereas the first shock was to wake ourselves up from the drunken state we were in at the bar, drunk on all sorts of illusions about ourselves, the second shock we need is the one that lifts us up to the next level so we can take control of the carriage. This shock involves getting ourselves together so we can feed the horse, repair the carriage, and fix or replace the tattered reins attaching the horse to the carriage. In other words, once we get out of the basement of our lives and into the open air, (the next level), we must then get our lives together so that we can operate in this world.

We spoke earlier of the Good Householder. He is the one who has made it in the world in the sense that he earns his living, has developed some skills, and is respected in the community for these abilities. Yet if this Good Householder has developed a Magnetic Center, he somehow realizes that this is not enough. Life is never going to answer his problems. Although he is part of life, he does not believe in it. He becomes open to distinguishing between A influences coming from life and B influences coming from esoteric sources outside of life. If he rises to this level, he can climb up to the box. As pointed out before, most of us are not at all interested in B influences and have no interest in esoteric teachings and therefore would not recognize them even if we were in the midst of them. If you have read this far, you are obviously interested in B influences.

Another interpretation of climbing up to the box is that before we can climb up to the box, we have to go down a level. We have to realize that we can do nothing and that we need help. We realize by self-observation that we are machines because we constantly act in the same way to external events. We don't want to be machines any longer. Who would want to be a machine always reacting in the same automatic, mechanical way? Therefore, we realize that we are in prison and we need someone to help us get out. This idea that we have to go down from where we are really living in order to rise is expressed in a simple Shaker spiritual that has become world famous, entitled, *Tis a Gift to be Simple*. It goes as follows, although some renditions vary:

Tis a gift to be simple,

Tis a gift to be free,

Tis a gift to come down to where we ought to be,

And when we come down to the place just right,

It will be in the valley of love and delight.

When true simplicity is found,

To bow and to bend,

We will not be ashamed.

To turn and to turn will be our delight,

Till by turning and turning

We come round right.

If we can make our personality passive and our essence active, perhaps, we can come to a place where, although others think we have become simple like the Shakers, we feel much better about ourselves. It is also interesting that the last line of the song refers to turning and turning to come round right and that there is a branch of the Sufis called the Whirling Dervishes who practice turning as a spiritual practice. Gurdjieff had his students doing all sorts of dance movements, including turning to "come round right." The Shakers themselves got their name from some of their movements, including actually shaking.

To get up to the box, we need to give ourselves the command, "I will drive." However, even if we give ourselves this command we still may not get up to the box. We will fall down or fail in various ways to reach the box. The Work stresses that it takes many efforts and many years of hard work before we can lift ourselves up. The Work is anything but a quick fix.

Once we do get up to the box, having fed the horse, repaired the carriage, and fixed the reins, and hold the reins in our hands ready to go, we come to the final and most important character in the parable. We may be sitting on the box ready to go, but the question is, where are we going? Only the master who now appears in the carriage can give us directions that we must obey as to where to go. The master is our Real 'I', and the whole object of the Work is to establish our Real 'I'. Of course, the master or Real 'I' doesn't appear in the carriage immediately.

There is a whole series of steps before the master or Real 'I' appears. The first is the Observing 'I'. The only way we can ever change ourselves is to see how we are at present. It is easy to observe how other people behave; it is a thousand times more difficult to observe how we act. That is why the beginning of the Work starts with self-observation. We have to observe ourselves and make mental photographs of how we act in all sorts of situations with others and when we are by ourselves. The most important aspect of this self-observation is that it be non-critical.

Once we have observed all our various 'I's and cluster of 'I's, the next step up in our development is the creation inside of us of a Deputy Steward, a manager of those 'I's who want to do the Work. This is a very important step because, instead of just having conflicting 'I's, each claiming to speak for us, the Deputy Steward can select which 'I' shall be in the driver's seat. We may feel low, but if we have committed ourselves to read a book or go to a meeting, the Deputy Steward will direct us to the proper task. Even having a Deputy Steward does not mean we no longer fall asleep. We still do, but the Deputy Steward helps us to awaken from our sleep-state.

The next step up is the Steward. The Steward comes from a higher source and, whereas the Deputy Steward will look after our household affairs, the Steward controls all our affairs. We develop a different sense of ourselves when we have a Steward guiding us. Above the Steward comes the Master or Real 'I'. The chief aim of the Work is to reach the Master or Real 'I'. In our drunken state in the public house, our imagination produced an Imaginary 'I' to hide our weaknesses and make us think we have unity and can do. In reality only the master, our Real 'I', can do, has unity and is awake.

All of esotericism is to awaken man from his drunken state and make him realize he is asleep as he is. Once he becomes Master (his real 'I'), he can direct the driver to go in the direction of awareness fully conscious of where he is going. So the hero of this parable is the Master who comes on the scene only after the driver has awakened from his drunken sleep with all the illusions he suffers from while in that state. I am a beginning student who is struggling to establish a Deputy Steward. I have not experienced the higher states. There is another aspect to this parable that is extremely important to the Work because it discusses the different bodies of man.

The Four Bodies of Man

According to the Work and other esoteric systems, we are capable of having four bodies. The first body, the physical one, is all we need to get through life. There is no need for the development of any other bodies. The physical body governs all our functions and in turn is governed by external influences of life. When we just have the first body and things go well for us in the external world, we are happy; when things go poorly for us externally, we are unhappy. We react automatically to the incoming impressions. This physical body is also called the Carnal Body, the "Corporal Body" in Christian terminology, and the first body in the Work. In the Parable of the Horse and Carriage, the first body is the carriage.

What the Work calls the second body is called the "Natural Body" in Christian terminology. In the parable, the second body is the Horse. Its chief characteristics are feelings and desires. With just a physical body or first body, our desires are produced automatically from the various 'I's we have that are often contradictory to each other. Even when we are successful in obtaining some desire, instead of feeling contentment and peace, new desires spring up from the same or different 'I's that keep us from achieving contentment or enjoying what we have achieved.

The Work states that each higher body controls the lower bodies. The second body controls the first body, and the third body controls the second and first bodies. As to how the second body is developed, the Work uses the analogy of a jar filled with various powders of different colors. If we shake the jar, the powders will all be dispersed. What was on top may move to the bottom, what was on the bottom may move to the middle. The essential characteristic of these powders as they relate to one another is their instability. There is no way to stabilize these powders in any particular manner. The Work states this is analogous to the first body, where the various 'I's are often contradictory and there is no stability. Stability can be brought to the various colored powders if a flame is applied to the jar holding these powders. The heat will fuse them and stability will be established. No matter how one tilts the jar, the colored powders will stay in the same position to one another; they have been fused.

As to how we can develop a second body that does not have all our contradictory 'I's and a permanent 'I' formed, heat must also be applied. The friction to be applied is the struggle between "yes" and "no". If we always react in the same way to external circumstances, we will always remain the same. If we give in to our habitual mode of reaction, we are saying, "yes" to our old ways. For example, we misplace something and always become angry. When we become angry we are giving in to our old ways of reacting, and nothing changes. On the other hand, if we can self remember when we misplace something, we can change our reaction from the usual habitual response. On the external side, we can see the keys have been misplaced, but internally we can also see that getting mad about it is not going to do us any good and will only make us lose force—so we say to ourselves, "Getting angry doesn't do anything but make me lose force. I know I will be fine one way or another."

If we can say "no" often enough, something new will be happening in us. We will be developing a second body. This second body will be much more organized than the chaos of the contradictory 'I's of the first body. We will have more unity and fewer contradictions than the first body. According to the Work, to develop a second body takes a long time. First the student must gain knowledge in the form of new ideas that can make the person think in new ways. Then the student must apply these new ways of thinking in the struggle between "yes" and "no" in the way that the student habitually and automatically reacts to external events.

There is one more point that is critical in establishing the second body. If only every once in a while you resist your inclination to get mad when you misplace your keys or a favorite item, it would never create the heat for a lasting change. Of course, any time you say "no" to your inclination to express negative emotions is good. It is a start, but for lasting change and to change your being, your efforts must be continuous and consistent. This is why change is so difficult and why we must be very patient with ourselves. No matter how often we fail, the critical point is that we don't give up but keep trying.

As to the development of the third body, if we heated the jar to a very high temperature, the mixture of the powders would not only stabilize but could take on new properties. It could become a solid, or radiate heat, or become radioactive, and so on. The process of imparting new properties to the fused alloy corresponds to the formation of the third body in man. We have established certain new qualities; we remember ourselves more; we have fewer contradictory

'I's; we are more able to hold to our aim, and so on. The problem is that these new properties can still be taken away by the same or different influences. The process of fixing these acquired new qualities so they can no longer be taken away is the development of the fourth body. It is through the fourth body that the Master 'I' (also consciousness and will) works. The man who has four fully developed bodies has many qualities that the other bodies don't have, including immortality. According to the Work, only a man who has developed the four bodies can be considered immortal. The fourth body is considered the divine body and the seat of immortality.

To me, the third and fourth bodies are very speculative. As someone who is still in the early stages of struggling in the battle between "yes" and "no", any body higher than the second body is highly academic. The main point, however, is that anyone who has developed a second body, or is in the process of developing one, has his actions determined more internally, rather than always being moved by life's events. He has more inner control over how he feels regardless of the life events that come to him. To use the terms of the American sociologist David Reisman in his 1950 book, *The Lonely Crowd*, he is inner-directed rather than outer-directed.

Moreover, and very importantly, the man with a second body realizes the life events he presently faces are exactly what he needs to work on with Work concepts such as nonidentifying. The life events are not exceptions to his smoothly running life, but are the actual material that is precisely meant for him to apply Work principles to. This is quite different from a man with only the first body, whose life is dominated by external events and whose happiness is always dependent on them. If he finds a twenty dollar bill he is happy; if he loses a twenty dollar bill, he in unhappy. He is always at the whim of life. Since life is a series of ups and downs, the Work says man can never win in life, and his life is a roller coaster going from happiness to unhappiness.

So the key issue is by what methods we can start to develop a second body. There are other aspects of the Work that ask the same questions in different contexts. For example, how can we, who are asleep as we are, even make the attempt to awaken? How can we raise our level of consciousness? How can we raise our level of being?

Methods for Awakening

Richard Liebow, a late friend, was a student and teacher of the Work for many years and had weekly group meetings in San Francisco for over ten years. Below is a list of some of the methods that were recited at each of his group's meetings:

1. Attend meetings;
2. Study chapter;
3. Prepare report;
4. Pause frequently just to be present;
5. Struggle to control the expression of negative emotions;
6. Practice dividing attention;
7. Verify ideas and methods;
8. Ask yourself, "Where am I in all this?"
9. Curb internal considering;

10. Cultivate external considering;

11. Scrutinize speech and try to control it;

12. Scrutinize habits and try opposing them;

13. Distinguish between the Work of the different function centers;

14. Direct attention to specific tasks;

15. Reconstruct experiences and events;

16. Prioritize and reprioritize;

17. Practice intensely active thinking by isolating issues and doing things in the order of their importance;

18. Observe mood swings;

19. Systematically release excessive muscular tension;

20. Define and redefine personal aims and purposes;

21. Strive to identify, transform and utilize A and B influences;

22. Question motives: Are they coming from an informed deputy steward—or from the false personality of a mad machine?

23. Make mental photographs—of postures, attitudes, gestures, breathing, and bodily sensations;

24. Observe and struggle to inhibit the tendency to procrastinate and make excuses;

25. And frequently ask yourself, "What will it matter a hundred years from today?"

Liebow had his students memorize this list of 25 methods. The listing is broken down into three groups of seven and the remaining group of four. I have memorized this list and found it is very helpful if I repeat it each morning. It reminds me of the principles of the Work, and I sometimes catch myself violating one of these methods and correct myself. I agree with Liebow's idea that memorizing lists helps focus the mind. I have found this to be very true for me in memorizing the 25 methods and reciting them to myself on my morning walks. The mind tends to be scattered and memorizing reigns the mind in and forces it to concentrate on a specific object, perhaps as a magnifying glass focuses the sun's rays on a particular object rather than dispersing the light over a wider area.

Some of these methods are self-explanatory, and others have been discussed earlier in the book. There are several methods that I believe warrant further discussion now in our attempt to awaken. I will discuss these rules in the context of how I started my own group and have interspersed some of my ideas within these 25 methods.

Attend meetings. This is the first one listed and is perhaps the most important. Gurdjieff and Ouspensky believed that the Work could not be done alone but required belonging to a group. I know I get much more from our reading in a group than when I read by myself at home.

Furthermore, nothing can be accomplished without a commitment, and this commitment takes conscious effort. Regular attending of meetings is one of the best ways to keep on track or bring us back on track if we have veered from the course. This principle applies to any type of program we may have adopted for our personal development, whether it is the AA program, another 12-step program, or any other program to which we have committed ourselves. This principle also applies to any type of physical activity, whether it is a yoga, Tai Chi, or weight training. Those who get the most out of these programs are the ones who attend regularly and do what the particular discipline requires.

The theory I go by is that each weekly meeting or physical activity session is like a drop in a bucket. At first we don't see anything in the bottom of the bucket, but very slowly as we continually go, drops accumulate and eventually we start to see some water at the bottom. We are starting to make gains in whatever program we have committed ourselves to.

On the other hand, if we go sporadically, the drops at the bottom of the bucket will evaporate, and we will always be starting from scratch. The idea that going to a weekend seminar in any field is a substitute for the weekly meetings or regular physical activity is an illusion. It is like filling the bucket to the brim during the weekend, and then on the way out the door or on the drive home, kicking the bucket and having nothing left in it. Of course, if there is no weekly meeting available to us, then going to a weekend seminar is the best we can do. If we could develop meetings in our hometown we would be better off than going sporadically to a weekend seminar.

Part of the Work is to keep going to these meetings despite the resistance when we don't feel up to going. Here, method 24 can be useful to recall. It states, "Observe and strive to inhibit the tendency to procrastinate and make excuses." To me, having a weekly meeting is like a weekly shock. No matter how far I have gone off course in the week, the readings we do in my own group always help me back toward the Work and waking up, even if it is just a miniscule amount.

This brings up the content of a meeting in a Gurdjieff group. I would say that there is no definite pattern of what a meeting should be like. It all depends on the group's leader. I attended several of Richard Liebow's groups in San Francisco: they consisted, at least partially, of memorizing lists, particularly the lengthy outlines of the chapters in Ouspensky's book, *In Search of the Miraculous*, and is very different from most groups. However, there are many ways to build a house, and as long as the builder knows what he is doing he will build a sound house. So I am sure that each competent Gurdjieff/Ouspensky leader will get results with his students. Of course, I think the student must find a leader that he feels he can work with. I do have some reservations about belonging to just any group.

Prepare reports was Liebow's third method. I think this is a crucial step because to understand the Work it must be applied to our lives. It is not something like learning Spanish where we add a new field of knowledge to ourselves. It is supposed to actually change our very being. How do we know when we have changed our being? The answer is that we react differently to the external events that happen in our lives. Only by changing our reactions can we change our level of being. Therefore, to record any change of reactions is the heart of working on ourselves. If we have to report back to others specific instances where we have applied the Work principles in our life, that gives us an added motivation to do the Work. Ultimately, the only real motivation, according to the Work, is our internal state that realizes the importance of practicing these principles whether or not we report our efforts to others.

At the weekly meetings I formed, the first question we ask after saying the invocation is, "How has your week gone, and have you made any efforts to do the Work in the last week?" Then we each relate our experiences, if indeed we have made efforts, and sometimes we simply draw a blank.

A Caveat on Group Leaders

Before proceeding further I would like to give my own personal warning about group leaders. Although the commonly held thought in the Work is that we need a teacher to escape the prison we are in. I personally think that being in a group studying the Work is extremely important, if not essential. I feel very comfortable about the group I formed for several reasons. There is no leader in the group; decisions are agreed upon by everyone, even changing the day of the weekly meeting because of a national holiday. We also agree together when we have read enough of the book for that night. There is no charge for our meetings.

The only cost, if people want to stay in the group, is to eventually buy their own copy of the Nicoll volume we are currently reading. We do not proselytize. If someone comes to a group and never shows up again, no one calls them to ask why they haven't come back. We have no business meetings, no socials, no potlucks, but sometimes a few members stay after the official meeting is over to socialize. We have a two-line ad in a free alternative monthly, *Sentient Times*, that covers Northern California and Southern Oregon, which simply says, "Gurdjieff-Ouspensky Study Group. Free Meetings.

Monday 6:00 p.m. to 7:30 p.m." Since we do not charge for our meetings, the paper generously does not charge us anything for placing the ad.

I discuss this because I think many groups, whether Gurdjieff or any other, can easily become manipulative and exploitive. Power corrupts and absolute power corrupts absolutely can happen in any group. In my experience, in most groups of people with three or more members, politics start to come into play, whether it is a couple of waitresses arguing about who has the best station, or truck drivers jockeying to get the best routes or hours. First comes politics, then comes socializing, and only then comes the actual work that the group was originally planning to do—whether it be to promote peace or war.

I have been around a few big time group leaders in areas outside the Work, and I wasn't impressed. For myself, I would never be able to stay in these situations where I could be bossed around. This is probably my defect but it just made me want to form a group where we stick to the essential of studying the Work without getting swamped with committees and power plays.

The group that I helped create is helping me, and I think we all have to feel comfortable in the group. If you are in a group and you feel manipulated, exploited or involved in a web of political intrigue, I would recommend getting out of that group, no matter how highly the leader is esteemed. To me it is also not important how big the group is. For over a year and a half our group consisted of Elaine and me. Elaine said that was fine with her, and it was fine with me. We could go on forever as a two-person group. If others joined us, that was fine, but we weren't concerned about the size of the group. To me the heart of the group is being in contact with the Work, and the main tool I see for that is reading out loud from books concerning the Work.

As to "official" Gurdjieff groups with a teacher, they exist in many major cities in America and Europe, and there are also groups on the Internet. For me, I prefer to go to a group and have it "live."

The Power of Reading Out Loud

I thought the best way to hold a meeting would be to read the actual words of someone who was a teacher. Since my group initially consisted of two people who had both read *In Search of the Miraculous* at least a few times, we both agreed that it was one of the major books of the Work, and agreed to start at the beginning and continue to the end. We had no set amount of pages to read at each session, but would read until we came to the end of a section. We would continue where we left off at the next meeting. In this way we completed the book in about a year.

Although I am an avid reader, for study purposes, the difference between reading silently and reading out loud is enormous. It is almost like reading a different book. We miss so much when we read silently—and the faster we read, especially a book as dense in content as Ouspensky's, the more we miss. This reminds me of Woody Allen's comment after he took a speed-reading course and read Tolstoy's novel *War and Peace* in eight minutes. When someone asked him what the novel was about, Allen replied, "Russia." To see what one misses, even in writing a simple letter, many people have had the experience of reading a letter out loud that they have written. As they read it, they catch all sorts of typos that they missed when they went over the letter silently. That there is a power in reading out loud is obvious when we consider we are using both our eyes and ears to take it all in. Sometimes I also run my finger along the line I am reading out loud to help keep my place, which adds another sense modality—touch—to the reading process.

As to the enjoyment of reading out loud, one need not go further than watching the delight of a child who is being read to. I first started reading to my daughter, Shona, the book *Goodnight Moon*. I don't know how many times I read that book, but it was many, many times. Shona never tired of it. It was a delight each time, as were other books, as she grew older.

There is one other advantage of reading out loud. When we read silently, we can read for a while and then realize we were just reading mechanically and not remember one single idea or event that took place in the sentence, paragraph, page, or chapter. Although we can read out loud mechanically and have our mind on other matters, this is much less likely to happen if we read out loud to someone else. Moreover, if we read out loud and omit a word such as the word "not" in a sentence, the listener can correct us and prevent us from distorting the meaning of what was written.

If you can find a group, I suggest you start to read one of the books in the Work out loud to someone else, and if you can't find someone else, read a few pages out loud to yourself. I would say that besides enjoyment, we get more out of a book by reading out loud than we do reading silently, just as we see more when we are walking than when we are driving.

Workbooks

I am of the opinion that it is better to read one book one hundred times than to read one hundred books once. The trick is to find the right book. I highly recommend Maurice Nicoll's *Psychological Commentaries on the Teachings of Gurdjieff and Ouspensky*. This is a five-volume set numbering 1766 pages with a sixth volume that is an index of the five volumes. Nicoll points out that his books are commentaries on the Work of Gurdjieff and not the true source of the Work.

The books consist of transcriptions of Nicoll's talks, given during and after the Second World War, and are incredibly clear and conversational in tone. Each chapter is just a few pages long. The ideas of the Work are woven throughout the five volumes into a fabric that repeats themes over and over again from different angles so that no stone is unturned in bringing these ideas out. If we could read only one book about the Work, I recommend the first volume of Nicoll's commentaries. It can be ordered from any local bookstore.

It could be argued that reading Gurdjieff or Ouspensky would be closer to the Work than reading Nicoll. Gurdjieff's writings are under the name *All and Everything*. It is a trilogy consisting of (1) *Beelzebub's Tales to His Grandson: An Objectively Impartial Criticism of the Life of Man* (All and

Everything, First Series); (2) *Meetings With Remarkable Men* (All and Everything, Second Series) and (3) *Life is Real Only When "I Am"* (All and Everything, Third Series.) All are available in paperback. As to the order of reading Gurdjieff's books, on the first page of *Life Is Real Only When "I Am",* Gurdjieff states that no one interested in his writings should ever attempt to read them in any order other than the one so indicated. In other words, the reader should never read anything written by Gurdjieff before he is already well acquainted with the earlier works.

From my perspective as a beginning student of the Work, I have been reading *Beelzebub's Tales to His Grandson*, but would never recommend it as an introduction to a beginning student of the Work. *Meetings With Remarkable Men* is very interesting, especially the last chapter entitled The Material Question, concerning how Gurdjieff developed his economic skills of earning a living and forming his organization. I don't think, however, it is a good systematic basis for studying the principles of the Work. I would say the same thing about Gurdjieff's *Life Is Real Only When "I Am."* There is also the book, *Views from the Real World: Early Talks of Gurdjieff as Recollected by His Pupils*. This is also available in paperback and is fairly readable for a beginning student of the Work.

As to Ouspensky's books, *In Search of the Miraculous* is one of the classics of the Work. It covers Ouspensky's initial meeting with Gurdjieff and quotes Gurdjieff extensively throughout the book. *The Fourth Way* consists of questions that people asked

177

Ouspensky after lectures and his answers. *The Psychology of Man's Possible Evolution* consists of the transcriptions of five talks written by Ouspensky and later read by his students to other people interested in the Work. The book also includes a brief autobiographical sketch. I highly recommend all of these books, and all are available in paperback. They are excellent and I have read them all at least a few times. For starters, *The Psychology of Man's Possible Evolution* might be the place to begin because it is a short overall introduction to the Work. Ouspensky, however, is sometimes not the easiest writer to follow and is a bit intimidating at times, such as when you see a complicated diagram of some aspect of the Work in *In Search of the Miraculous*. Ouspensky also wrote a novel entitled, *The Life of Ivan Osokin*, as well as *Talks with a Devil and Conscience: The Search for Truth.*

As to other sources of the Work, many students of Gurdjieff and Ouspensky later became teachers of the Work and wrote books about it and/or their relationship with Gurdjieff and Ouspensky. A partial list of these students and some of the books they wrote (most of which I have not read yet) follows: J. G. Bennett, *Is there Life on Earth?* and *Energy*; Robert Burton, *Self-Remembering*; Robert DeRopp, *The Master Game*; Fritz Peters, *My Boyhood with Gurdjieff* and *My Journey with a Mystic*; A. L. Stavely, *Memories of Gurdjieff*; Rodney Collins, *Theory of Celestial Influences, Theory of Eternal Life, and Mirror of Light*; Kathryn C. Hulme, *Undiscovered Country: In Search of Gurdjieff*; Kathleen Riodan Speeth, *The Gurdjieff Work*; Ira Friedlanden, *Gurdjieff: Seeker of the Truth*; Jan Cox, *Dialogues of Gurdjieff*; C.S. Natt, *Further Teachings of Gurdjieff, Journey Through the World*, and *The Journal of a Pupil*; James Webb, *The Harmonious Circle*; Alfred Orage, *Psychological Exercises*; and Maurice Nicoll, who, in addition to *The Commentaries*, wrote *Living Time, The New Man* and *The Mark*. In addition to these followers who became teachers and wrote books, Gurdjieff had many students, such as William Niland, who never wrote any books but whose audiotapes are available. Gurdjieff also attracted many well-known people as students such as the author Katherine Mansfield, whose book *Journal of Katherine Mansfield* discusses the Work, and the Russian musician Thomas de Hartmann.

Conclusion

If you have come this far in this book, I want to point out what should be rather obvious by now: this is not an easy system. No one can make the effort for you. It's up to you. There is a salvation, but it isn't gained merely by believing in God or a higher level of consciousness. Although this belief is necessary to commence the Work, it is only the beginning of the task. The salvation lies in doing the Work ourselves on ourselves so we can raise our level of being. No one will be carrying us on his or her back, and there is no quick fix. It takes years of study, feeling the Work emotionally, and then applying it by observing how we behave, and struggling to change our reactions to life rather than trying to change the circumstances of our external life. In fact, the Work says that whatever is currently going on in our lives is exactly what we need to work on. The Work all depends on our understanding. Only understanding and then applying this understanding to our lives will change things.

The analogy Gurdjieff used was that of an onion. We have to keep taking off layers of the onion (our personality) to get to our Real 'I' (our essence). To change our being, essence must start to grow and become active, and personality must become passive. This is perhaps analogous to a butterfly emerging from its cocoon. Our essence is the butterfly trying to break through the cocoon that surrounds it, which is our personality. Each time we remember ourselves, we connect with our essence and therefore with eternity. Personality, which was developed by life, wants us to identify constantly with every situation life thrusts upon us. Personality keeps us in a constant state of identification, going from one problem to another. We are always losing force, and we cannot develop ourselves and increase our level of being. The Work says that we are all experiments on this Earth and that we are self-developing organisms. Whether we develop depends on our conscious efforts to do the Work.

There is a story of a man watching a butterfly breaking through its cocoon. After much effort, the butterfly's one wing broke through the cocoon. The butterfly kept working to get the other wing out. After watching for a longer time than it took for the first wing to break out, the man observing the butterfly thought he could help and pricked the cocoon on the side. The second wing came out, but it was deformed.

The only person who can do the Work is ourselves. In a sense we must cleanse ourselves of ourselves. No one can observe our internal lives, states, attitudes, or postures but ourselves. Teachers can give us new ideas and information, which is important, but this information will just be mere accumulation of facts, if not applied. The only way to make the Work functional is to actually apply it by observing ourselves uncritically. We are the subjects of this Work. The aim of the Work is not to change the world but to change ourselves.

I would like to conclude by quoting a man who also developed a philosophical system to transform himself. Because of his beliefs, at the age of twenty-four he was ostracized from the Jewish community in Amsterdam. He lived by himself, earning his living grinding lenses, and died at the age of forty-five. His philosophy gave him a wonderful disposition. He turned down all sorts of honors in his life such as becoming a professor at prestigious universities. His name was Baruch Spinoza. He lived from 1632 to 1677. His best-known book, *Ethics*, was published posthumously in 1677. I believe the note at the end of his book gives a cogent description of the results of his philosophy and the difficulties of obtaining it. I think it is appropriate to end my book with the last line of Spinoza's final note: "If salvation lay ready to hand and could be discovered without great labor, how could it be possible it should be neglected almost by everybody? But all noble things are as difficult as they are rare."

Reviews of Other Books by Gil Friedman

How to Be Totally Unhappy in a Peaceful World: A Complete Manual with Rules, Exercises, a Midterm and a Final Exam

"This is a good book when one feels down and needs an uplift. It allows one to realize not to take life so seriously. Very enjoyable reading." —*Judy, Amazon.com*

"From the Acknowledgements up front to the blurbs on the back cover, there are unexpected fits of laughter awaiting you in this clever little book. It is an extended parody on self-help books, human nature, and our frenetic, outer-orientated society . . . this wise clever, and exceedingly funny book is a gem." —*Arcata Eye* (Arcata, CA)

"It is a wonderful look at humans and the ways we think and act. I found it to be saddening, enlightening and funny all at the same time . . . . I'm sure everyone will find something they can relate to from their lives past, present or future." —*North Coast Co-op News*

"I absolutely love this book! What may at first glance appear to be an exercise in frustration is actually an ingenious exploration of the human condition and what we can do, or avoid doing, in order to enjoy life. Though the shelves may be filled with innumerable self-help, how to and spiritual guidance books all telling you how to live your life, Gil flips the tale on its head. This book is one of the only I have seen that offer suggestions as to what one could avoid and leaves open to the reader the possibilities of what may be. It does so in such a way that is witty and wonderful with satire and wisdom. I highly recommend this book to anyone interested in exploring the ways we can be and navigating the layers of reality."
—*Amazon.com*

(It had been translated into Spanish, Danish, Thai and Chinese.)

191 Pages, 30 illustrations; four pages of cartoons by renowned cartoonist. 6" by 9" Trade paperback.
ISBN 0-913038-12-1   Yara Press   Price: $16.95

Love Notes: Quotations from the Heart

An expanded version of my book formerly entitled *A Dictionary of Love*. Over 650 quotations on love from the profane to the profound arranged alphabetically into 211 subject categories by over 350 authors. Complete with authors' index and bibliography.

"I gave this book to my husband for Valentine's Day and he loved it! The quotes are thoughtful, funny, inspiring and diverse. Sometimes the juxtaposition of the quotes themselves is humorous. Many of the quotes ring a note of profound wisdom and I often find myself thinking as I read, "Yes, how true!" Of course, the topic is immense and here it's covered from various aspects, A to W, in an organized, easy to use manner. I imagine writing this was a labor of love and probably compiled over years of reading on the topic. Our copy now resides the bathroom and makes for wonderful, quick reading. You can open the book anywhere and find some hearty nugget to laugh at or ponder. A delight to read, it makes a great gift too." —*Kathleen, Amazon.com*

"(A) terrific book. . .Funny, rueful, practical, wise and compassionate. . .Lots of fun, and more educational than many a tome." —*New Age Retailer*

"A really fun book to read. There's either a good laugh or a real thought-provoker (or even both) on each page." —*New England Bride*

"Witty, profound and sometimes just plain fun." —*American Reference Book Annual*, Vol. 22; Libraries Unlimited, Inc.

(It has been translated into Korean and Chinese)

ISBN 9130338-00-8
5 ½" by 7 ½" Trade Paperback
209 pages
Yara Press
Price $12.95

Excerpts of all books can be found at
www.GilFriedman.com

To order, call (707) 822-5001 or send $22 for another copy of this *Gurdjieff* book; $16 for *Love Notes*; or $18 for the *Unhappy* book; or all three for $50 (all prices include handling and any applicable taxes) to Gil Friedman, Yara Press, 1735 J Street, Arcata, CA 95521.

Lightning Source UK Ltd.
Milton Keynes UK
UKOW052002080413

208885UK00014B/1271/P